Appreciation and interpretation of Religion in the Modern Age

Asr-E Hazir Men Din ki Tafhim Aur Tashrih
(At Tafsir-us-Siyasi Lil-Islam)

Abul Hasan Ali Nadwi

Translated By
Syed Athar Husain

NADWI PRESS

NADWI PRESS

Nadwi Press
First Published in 1982
New Edition - 2023 CE - 1445 H

Translation of the Qur'ān

It should be perfectly clear that the Qur'ān is only authentic in its original language, Arabic. Since perfect translation of the Qur'ān is impossible, we have used the translation of the meaning of the Qur'ān throughout the book, as the result is only a crude meaning of the Arabic text.

Qur'ānic verses appear in speech marks proceeded by a reference to the Surah and verse number. Sayings (Hadith) of Prophet Muhammad (saw) appear in inverted commas along with reference to the Hadith Book and its Reporter.

CONTENTS

★★★

Translator's Note

This translation of the book *'Asr-e hazir men Din ki Tafhim aur Tashrih'* has been done at the behest of its author, Maulana Saiyid Abul Hasan Ali Nadwi, for whom I have the greatest regard for his erudition, profundity of knowledge, scholarship and oratory and for his dignified but extremely unassuming personality. I have been associated with him for two decades as also with his Academy of Research and Publication, Nadwatul Ulama which has published some of my important books, namely. *Prophet Muhammad and his Mission, the Glorious Caliphate, the Message of al-Quran, the Book of Thousand Lights* and a few others which by grace of God have gained international fame. At the moment it is arranging publication of my book on Islamic mysticism.

I have also great regard for the unique personality and sterling qualities of Maulana Saiyid Abul Ala Maududi and have great admiration for his translation and commentary of the Holy Quran. Even so, I totally disagree with Maulana Maududi's thesis as presented in his book '*The Four Basic Quranic Terms* and completely agree with what Maulana Saiyid Abul Hasan Ali has written in this volume.

I do not wish to repeat the arguments put forward by Maulana Nadwi for, firstly it is not at all necessary and secondly, I cannot do it as well as he has done. Nevertheless, I am venturing to give some of my own comments. To those who have not read my books, I have to say that having written over two dozen books on various aspects of Islam, I should be expected to know something about Islam and Islamic history.

The first observation that I have to make is that when any scholar, howsoever distinguished he may be, has to say something about history or historical development he has to cite the authority on the basis of which he is making the statements or generalisations, particularly in the event of serious departure from the accepted view coming down through the ages. Maulana Maududi says that every one in Arabia knew the meaning and import of the four basic terms of the Quran, viz., *'Ilah'*, *'Rab'*, *'Din'* and *'Ibadat'* at the time of the advent of the Quran, but as centuries passed the real meaning of all these terms gradually underwent subtle changes so that, in course of time, instead of the full connotations they came to stand for only very limited meaning and restricted and rather vague concepts. According to him one reason was the gradual decline of interest in the Arabic language and the other that the words ceased to have the same meaning for the later generations of Muslims that they had for the original Arabs to whom the Quran had been revealed. It is for these two reasons that in the more recent lexicons and commentaries many of the Quranic words began to be explained not in their original sense but by what they had, by then, come to stand for e.g., the word *Ilah*, as used in respect of other than God, came to be synonymous with idols or gods; the word *'Rab'* came to mean only some one who brings up or rears or feeds another or provides for his worldly needs: *'Ibadah'* began to be understood as *'Puja'* or *'Prastish'* and *'Din'* as equivalent to *'Dharama'* or 'Religion'.

This assertion can be interpreted only to mean that as ages rolled on, people went on giving different meaning and import to these four basic terms. This is a very serious statement on which is based his entire theory. It has got to be examined very critically in the light of historical evidence but Maulana Maududi has cited no auhority to support the statment, although it was absolutely incumbent upon him to do so. If the meanings of these terms had gone on changing in different times it was incumbent upon him to state precisely what were the different meanings assigned to the terms in the various ages. To support such an assertion not one but a number of authorities are needed to describe the changes in the various ages. But Maulana Maududi has not cited a single authority for the simple reason that there is no such authority. He states that in the later day dictionaries and commentaries of the Quran, the Quranic words were interpreted not in the literal sense but as they were understood by the Muslims. What are those dictionaries and books of exegesis in which the terms were defined and interpreted in different ways Maulana Maududi does not mention.

Maulana Maududi has assigned two reasons for the supposed changes. One is lessening of taste for chaste Arabic and the other is admixture of other people in Muslim society. In putting forward his first reason, Maulana Maududi had probably only India in view. After the liquidation of the Mughal empire in India and its occupation by the British, lesser and lesser number of people learnt Arabic and there might have been even lessening of taste for chaste Arabic (though this could hardly be so in the case of people studying or teaching in well established Arabic institutions) but surely this could not happen and did not happen in the rest of the Islamic world barring probably Persia. In the Arabic speaking world Arabic, being the mother tongue and official language, could not register any decline. On the contrary, it continued to flourish and to be further and further enriched. The second reason is no reason at all. It is only in the nature of begging the question. In advancing it, Maulana Maududi was again probably influenced by the conditions prevailing in India. In what other Muslim countries of the world, with the possible exception of Persia, had other societies got mixed up with the Muslims? There were different races no doubt at the time of the advent of Islam even in Arabia, but they had all embraced Islam in the time of the Holy Prophet (peace be on him) or in the time of the illustrious caliphs. Then again, barring the last two or three centuries, when Muslims, like the rest of the world, were influenced by western civilisation and materialism it is the Muslims who had influenced the rest of the world in thc fields of literature, arts, science, philosophy, learning and knowledge. When materialism spread its tentacles, it had nothing to do with definitions of *'Ilah'*, *'Rab'*, *'Din'* or *'Ibadat'*. It bred irreligiosity and gave a wide berth to such terms with which it had no concern. To say that' *'Din'* was equated with *'Dharam'* or 'Religion' is nothing but cavilling at words.

These words might have been used by some people or in some Urdu dictionaries of recent times to explain the meaning of the Arabic words to people not knowing the language or the Islamic terms but surely such an explanation does not imply that the very meaning and significance of the words was lost to Muslims. *'Puja'* is a Hindi word meaning worship and *'Prastish'* is its Persian equivalent. We are not concerned with the form or object of *'Puja'* or *'Prastish'* but with the meaning of the terms. Furthermore, the terms *'Puja'* *'Prashtish'* or *'Dharam'* are unkonwn in the Arabic speaking Islamic countries and Maulana Maududi is talking about the whole world of Islam. The plain truth is that, very unfortunately, a distinguished scholar like Maulana Maududi has based his entire theory on preconceived notions and imaginary grounds and in propounding it has kept only India in his view. It lacks foundation, is unsupported by historical evidence and is even against common sense.

I would like to touch only two other aspeets of the matter about which much has been said by him, i.e. *tasawwuf* and the relationship between man and his Creator. The third theory that man-made laws have no relevance or validity is too absurd to comment upon it.

It has been very strongly advocated by Maulana Maududi that the relationship between man and his Creator is only of a subject and Sovereign and of a servant and his Master and Lord. Maulana Abul Hasan Ali and other luminaries of Islam, whom he has extensively quoted, have firmly established that while this relationship does exist for God Almighty is undoubtedly the sovereign and supreme Authority of the entire universe, but that is not the end of the matter. The relationship is infinitely wider, deeper and fuller and there is an ethereal quality about it. There are almost innumerable verses of the Quran that man has to obey his Lord and Master and to carry out His commands but at the same time he has to form a proper estimation of Him by fixing his gaze on the beauty of His manifestations, and regard Him as his real Benefactor, Friend, Guardian, Protector, Sustainer and Preserver and to have an intensely loving and emotional attachment with Him.

To limit the relationship between God and man to that of sovereign and his subjects or a lord and his servant is to miss the very meaning of religion. Religion is an integral part of man and is an eternal truth intrinsically woven into the fabric of human life. It is man's response to the presence and appeal of an unknown world that evokes his awe, reverence and confidence. It is the reaction of man's whole being to the object of his highest loyalty. It is to be felt and thought, it is to be lived and translated into action. In fact, it is a vital personal experience. Islam does not mean only servitude but total submission to God in beliefs, feelings, emotions, thoughts and actions. It covers every sector of man's life, every segment of his being. It demands a living consciousness of God pulsating as a vibrant force in every sphere of his life. The more a man advances in the spiritual scale, stronger is his emotional and intellectual attachment with God till he reaches to close proximity with Him and becomes entirely His so much so that according to a Hadith Qudsi, God says, 'When I love him, I am to him an ear and a hand and a helper, through Me he hears, and through Me he sees and through Me he takes.

Islam is a religion of moderation entrusted to a "balanced community". It is not a dry and prosaic religion as some may be inclined to imagine. Its beauty, grandeur, appeal and sublimity are unsurpassable. It rests on eternal truths whose charm is captivating and exhilirating, It prescribes certain minimum acts of worship but it calls upon man to perform them in loving devotion and to respond from the depth of his heart. It is a celestial call of the infinity which sinks into the heart of man and permeates his whole being. There are numerous verses of the Quran and scores of *ahadith* calling upon man to love God with all the fervour at his command and to remember Him constantly in utter devotion and humility. Man is no doubt God's bondsman but a favourite bondsman, the highest of creation in whose service every object and force of nature has been pressed. He can fall to the lowest of the low but he can rise to the highest of the high.

I am amazed at the magnitude of misconception of *Tasawwuf* by Maulana Abul Ala Maududi. According to him it is an opiate, a later day accretion and, at the best, it falls in the category of permissibles but has to be eschewed as it breeds stagnation, defeatism and a flight from realities of life. As Maulana Abul Hasan Ali has amply proved there can be nothing farther from the truth. *Tasawwuf* is as old as Islam, nay, it was practised by all the prophets of the yore. It is the essence of faith and the soul of Islam. Its basic ingredients are conscious and living realisation of the unity of God *(Tauhid)* in all its implications, adoration and love of God, purification of the heart and righteousness. Its every ingredient is not only endorsed by Islam but constitutes the very base of the religion. It calls upon man to inculcate the qualities of piety, sincerity, trust in God, patience, steadfastness and gratitude to God. It should not be judged by the conduct of fakes and pretenders or the worldly sufis. If there are bad *Sufis*, so are there bad *Ulama* who are to be avoided according to a *Hadith*. *Tasawwuf* is such a vast, profound and sublime subject that one cannot even touch its fringes wtihin the span of few pages. Its depth and dimensions can be experienced but cannot be adequately describcd. It comprises purification of the *Nafs*, inculcation of the noblest qualities—a shadow of the attributes of God, attainment of love of God, certitude, His nearness and gnosis *(ma'rifat)*. When man reaches this state the reality of eternal values dawns upon him and a new horizon of the Beyond opens up before him. Then man begins to live in God and the reciprocated love is thrilling, captivating, ecstatic and all-absorbing. To deny the services of the great Sufi saints in establishment and expansion of Islam is to deny a patent and well-established truth and the whole history of Islam.

Establishment of religion is certainly understandable and it is the duty of every Muslim to contribute towards it. But it is not readily understood what is meant by establishment of kingdom of God for it has always been there from the very genesis of the world to the very minute of our existence. There was never a time when it was not there and it shall continue to remain till eternity. It governs every creation, every object whether animate or inanimate, in fact every atom of every thing and all the physical laws of nature. There is nothing outside it. However, if it means enforcement of ideals of equality, fraternity, liberty, equality and justice and the penal laws for curbing vices and sins, they are incorporated in the constitution and penal laws of every country. But if it means establishment of a theocratic state and enforcement of the penal laws of the *Shariat*, that can be done only in a Muslim state. There can be no greater calamity for Muslims than establishment of a theocratic state in a country predominantly peopled by followers of another religion.

In the end, I may mention that translations of the verses of the Quran have been taken from its English translation by Dr. Syed Abdul Latif.

Lucknow :
May 25, 1981.

SYED ATHAR HUSAIN.

★★★

PRESENTATION

THIS BOOK is presented to every dear friend who believes that the real objective of life is attainment of pleasure of God, action in accordance with the Book and Sunnat, admission in paradise and salvation in the Hereafter and that besides these every other endeavour in the way of religion, organisation and leadership of parties and reformation of social and political systems and governmental rule, are mere means and methods which are employed to attain this objective and the advancement and supremacy of Islam. For such a person attachment with personalities is for the sake of God, his interest and zeal in activities and organisations are intended to support and assist religion and do not arise from partisan feelings.

THE BOOK is offered to every one who believes that among the innumerable bounties of God which He bestows on mankind, there is only one bounty which has been withdrawn and that is prohethood after the Holy Prophet of Islam (peace be on him). All other bounties and munificence are still in operation like the bestowal of intelligence, insight and emotion and capacity for sound and extensive quest and finding. No one holds a monopoly for any of them nor the world has witnessed their end with the end of any person.

THIS BOOK is also a gift to those who seek progress and excellence and if they are convinced of some truths they do not hesitate to accept them. As Hazrat Umar said 'The real thing is truth and return to it is neither a matter of shame nor any thing unusual or extraordinary'.

THIS BOOK is also offered to those who believe that criticism and evaluation is a collective right which can be excercised by any body and no knowledgeable and competent person can be deprived of this right and soundness of criticism and fair expression of views are not like a civic rule directing one way traffic.

AND LASTLY, this book is presented to those who do not pass judgements on any book without reading and fully understanding it, nor impute motive on its authorship nor hasten to suspect the underlying purpose of it.

Says the Quran :–

> "Cheer with good tiding (O, Prophet !) those who listen to every thing but follow that is good therein ; it is such as these whom God guideth ; it is such as these who are men of insight"
>
> —(Q. 39 : 17, 18)

S. Abul Hasan Ali Nadwi

Foreword of the Second Edition

All Praise to the Lord of all Domains and salutation to the Holy Prophet.

This book "Appreciation and Interpretation of Religion in the Modern Age" was written in the Ramadhan of 1398 Hijri corresponding to August 1978 and it came out of the press in Ziqad 1398 Hijri, i.e. October 1978. Because of the importance of the subject, it quickly reached all corners of the country. On the insistence of some Arab friends of the author, it was decided to bring out an Arabic translation and the task was entrusted to Molvi Noor Alam Amini Nadwi, an adept translator of Arabic, who contributes regularly articles to tbe journals *'Al-Bath-al Islami'* and *'Ar-Rayed'* and is a lecturer in Darul-Uloom Nadwa. He did the job very capably but when the author went through it, he made a number of additions here and there, as is his wont, particularly in the Preface.

These additions were necessitated on going through letters received by the author largely from the rank and file of Jamat-e-Islami of India and a lesser number from its office bearers and more responsible persons betraying a severe emotional reaction over the book. Some letters went to the extent of doubting the motive of the author. They, however, contained some points which made it necessary to give fuller discussion of what had been set forth briefly in the preface of the Urdu edition. The author could not imagine that a balanced and careful criticism of a purely academic and thought-provoking character would invite expression of so much unpleasantness and severe reaction.

Shortly after the publication of the book, the author had sent a copy of it along with a personal letter to Maulana Saiyed Abul Ala Maududi which was acknowledged and replied by him in his letter of the 23rd January 1979 which was in every way befitting his great personality. He had written, interalia 'I have never considered myself above criticism nor do I take it ill'. He invited the author to analyse and assess his other works in the same detached manner and to communicate to him his *'reaction and doubts'*.

In bringing out the second edition of the book, the author thought it proper to include in it what had been added in the Arabic translation and this way the second edition has become more complete and useful. It Is hoped that this edition will not be passed over as reproduction of the first edition by those who have gone through the first edition.

The author is happy and thanks God that the book had come out in the life time of Maulana Saiyid Abul Ala Maududi and he had occasion to go through it. Had his death preceded its publication considerable hesitation would have been felt in publishing it and it could have evoked considerable misgivings and annoyance in certain quarters. It would have been difficult to counter or dispel that emotional reaction by logical arguments.

So far as the sterling qualities, accomplishments and services of the departed Maulana are concerned there was never any doubt about them. The author has acknowledged them at every occasion gladly and open-heartedly and threw light upon them in his article published in the journal *Tameer-e-Hayat* three or four days after his death. It forms part of his recent work entitled '*The Old Lamps*'. However, when he read the articles written by scholars having affiliations with his party, he found them, to his chagrin, in great contrast to the efforts of reformers against the cult of personality and the advice of Maulana himself. His conviction grew stronger that for any party, based on the writings and views of an individual, it is extremely hard to avoid partisanship and exaggerated veneration of the personality to the degree of sanctity.

In the Arabic version an article had been added under the caption of '*Ahda*' which has been incorporated in this book under the title of "Presentation".

I pray to God that the book may be read with the same sincerity of spirit which prompted its writing.

S. Abul Hasan Ali Nadwi

Daira Shah Alam Ullah,
Rai Bareli.

10 Ziqad 99 A.H.
2nd October, 1979

★★★

Preface to the First Edition

Islam is the final religion laid down by God. Till the Doomsday, the guidance and salvation of man are dependent upon it. Till then it has to stay for man's worldly and other worldly guidance. Its beliefs and truths are unchangeable and its instructions and commandments are irrevocable and unalterable. Not only its *Shariat*, but its culture and civilization are based on truths. At the same time it is also true that life is a continuous movement and development and changes and alterations take place in it. This is not its defect but a quality, it is not a departure from nature but is natural. It goes on changing its outer garment, languages, ways of thinking, reasons and causes inciting inner conflicts, the methods and means employed for their satisfaction, questions arising internally and their answers all go on changing.

In such a contradictory state when life is ephemeral and amenable to changes and truth and religion are eternal and permanent, it becomes incumbent upon the faithful, the interpreters and the exponents of religion to so interpret and explain it in the light of the eternal truths and beliefs that the hearts of the new generations are thrilled with renewed faith and their minds accept willing obedience. Hazrat Ali has very wisely said, "Converse with people according to the state of their intellectual capacity and mental development. Do you want them to resile from the truths of God and His Apostle by conversing with them at a level unintelligible to them."[1]

This was kept in view by all the great protagonists of Islam, the great savants and stalwarts of the various ages. We can mention the names of Imam Abul Hasan Ash'ari, Imam Abu Mansur Maturidi, Imam Ghazali, Imam Fakhruddin Razi, Saikh-ul-Islam Ibn Taimiya, the saint Rumi Maulana Jalaluddin of Konya, Hakim-ul-Islam Shah Waliullah of Delhi who discharged this obligation in various ways according to the needs of their times.

But this task is as delicate and difficult as it is essential. Great care has to be taken that the exposition and interpretation, the simplification and elaboration, the picture and fascimile are so carefully and nicely put forward that those of the new generation or groups who are to be acquainted with or to be convinced of basic truths and beliefs or who are to be utilised for propagation and establishment of religion do not lose that Islamic temper which was the distinguishing mark of the Prophets' preachings or their proliferation by the companions and was transmitted to succeeding generations. It has to be ensured that their thinking and efforts do not leave the tracks established by the august body as happened in the histories of religions or schism of Islam. This catastrophe takes place only once in the history of religions but when it does take place there is nothing to atone for it. The right religious temper is a divine gift and is the fruit of His assistance which is a distinguishing mark of prophethood. It is the most valuable treasure, the finest patrimony of the *Ummat* and in it lies its greatest strength and vitality and it has to be most deligently and scrupulously guarded. This temper can be spoiled but it cannot be restored without the help of prophetic preachings, the guidance of his instructions, and the

1. *Fath-ul-Mulhim, Sharah Sahih Muslim*, vol. I, p. 126

impact of pious and saintly company and training. Decadence of Islamic spirit or deflection from it cannot be steadied and atoned by even great govenmental authorities, political powers and organisations.

Because of the capable handling of this great and delicate task of interpretation and exposition in every age, there is not that wide gulf between this generation and Islamic beliefs, values and appreciation as has repeatedly arisen in the history of Christianity and Judaism between the educated and intelligent followers of those faiths and the teachings of the two religions. Initially this sector turned away in dissatisfaction from the teachings of the Bible and then it rose up in open revolt and in both the religions, irreligiosity and atheism raised their heads on an extensive scale which recoiled upon the world. In Islamic history the great exponents of religion did not allow such an eventuality to occur and the intellectual and philosophical links of the *Ummat* with Islamic beliefs and principles remained unbroken. On the contrary, they gained strength and tenacity in every age so that the community had never to face a predicament, like the Parsis and Hindus, that they stuck to religious and social customs but doubted and despaired of the ability of their religion to stand to intellectual analysis and to meet the challenges of the times and to helplessly let veils of superstitions and ignorance remain hanging over their religions to prevent exposure to rays of enlightenment for their own safety. The community should generously acknowledge the services of the interpreters and commentators of Islam and feel grateful to them that they saved it from the rivalry of learning and religion and the mortal conflict between the two which the world of middle ages witnessed in Christiandom and about which the great American scholar John William Drapper wrote his outstanding book, *Conflict between Religion and Science*.

The useful and auspicious work of exposition and interpretation continued in every age, by grace of God, through such dialecticians, commentators and exponents of Islam who deligently and successfully discharged their responsibility. Side by side, there were always present in the community learned men who themselves knew the real spirit of *Din* and *Shariat* and could feel the pulse of the new generations. They kept a critical eye on the contemporary interpretation and exposition to ensure that it did not outstep the patent path laid down by the Holy Prophet and that the current temper was not out of tune with the religion that has to serve as an ideal and standard till the end of the world. While fully appreciating the work of interpretation and without doubting the intentions of the interpreters, they gave expression to their candid opinions and pointed out mistakes and improprieties whenever they noticed them. They did not let the fame and popularity and high stations of the thinkers and men of knowledge and letters nor even their piety and sanctity to stand in the way and expressed their own views and reactions sincerely and in a balanced and dispassionate manner. The great scholars, thinkers and interpreters welcomed, without any constraint, the assessments of the sincere critics and utilised their suggestions to make their own efforts more useful, balanced and meaningful. From the very beginning of Islam there is a continuous chain of such servants and supporters of *Shariat* and according to the prophecy of a tradition it will continue till the end of the world. The Tradition says, "there will be in every age such just and righteous heirs and bearers of this learning who will continue removing the distortions introduced by men prone to exaggerations, spurious claims and presentations of the wicked and far-fetched explanations of the ignorant."[1]

The existence of both the groups is necessary. In their

1. *Mishkat—The Book of knowledge,* part II

collabotation and cooperation lies the safety of the religion and the continuation of the Islamic spirit and thinking.

From the beginning of the nineteenth century the increasing political power of the West, its spectacular conquests in the field of science and technology and its dominant material supremacy created a great mental tension in the world of Islam which had become a victim of intellectual depression, and political weakness and confusion.[1] If in earlier days interpretation and exposition of Islam in the contemporary world was a commendable job, it became later on a *kifaya* obligation. The young educated section, particularly those who had travelled in Europe near the end of the nineteenth century or at the beginning of the twentieth century or had contacts with English officers or western intellectuals began not only to doubt Islamic beliefs but rebelled against them and a large number succumbed to intellectual and cultural apostasy. At that juncture there came forward in various parts of the Islamic world men of letters and men of knowledge who tried to counter the onslaught by propogation of *Din,* Islamic *Shariat,* Isiamic culture and history, and its systems of government and education and rendered great service in the light of their own education, training and capabilities particularly in Turkey, Egypt, Syria and India. Though the work was not without usefulness and saved many a person from intellectual apostasy, these attempts had generally been defensive or apologetic in character. Some endeavoured to bridge the gap between European and Islamic culture and values and were inclined to temporize with European political and economic theories without reservation and to weave them over Islamic preachings and history. At places far-fetched explanations and exposition of Islam and its teachings could be seen which were

1. For knowing its development and its different states in different countries, one can see the author's book *Western Civilization, Islam and Muslims.*

calculated to make them correspond with established views of the West. The real stalwarts, however, while acknowledging the partial value of the attempts, made learned assessments and prevented adoption of the attitude which was bound to develop by such a literature and brought back the educated Muslim youth to the right path. The danger of universal deflection created by the 'researches' and writings of such men of letters was thus averted.

The most careful and solid work in this connection was done in India which, because of its subjugation by the British, had become the biggest field for the conflict between Islam and westernism and where, as a result of the prevalent religious educational system and cultural process and the influence of Sufis, Ulama and the Masters, the common man and the educated sector possessed power of resistance which was either non-existant or very weak in other Islamic or Arab countries. In addition, because of the war of independence in 1857 and its failure, the Khilafatagitation and the non-cooperation movement in the first quarter of the twentieth century, dislike and abhorrence against the British rule and the British race had developed which was the greatest representative and upholder of this civilization, thinking and way of life. That also stopped the Muslim from being swept away in the flowing European current of intellectual atheism and cultural apostasy. Resistance to western thinking and values was growing in its own way when in the first half of this century the articles of Maulana Saiyid Abul Ala Maududi published in his esteemed journal *Tarjumanul Qura'n* from Hyderabad, which were written not in any defensive but in an aggressive way against western civilisation and philosophy of life, attracted the attention of the educated Muslims. Those articles had confronted the movement of modernity bred by western education and had opposed rank nationalism. He also wrote powerful and well-reasoned articles on Islamic *Shariat* and Laws which had become the target of attack like usury, *purdah*, *jihad*, sacrifice, slavery, *Hadith* and *Sunnat*. Through those articles, which later on appeared in the shape of bound volumes, and his other books and treatises, he moulded the thinking of recipients of modern education and restored in them confidence in Islamic values and thinking and rescued them from any sense of inferiority or defeatism. That was sterling work indeed which must be acknowledged and because of it many men of letters gave him the title of 'Spokesman of Islam'.

It would have been a great good fortune of Islam and the Muslims, if he had made this work the purpose and objective of his life and a field for expression of his God-given talents. But alongside it he started the work of modernisation of Islamic thinking and reorientation of Islamic metaphysics and made it the instrument of Muslim awakening and the foundation of organisation and intellectual core of Jamat-e-Islami. I mean his famous and popular book The *Four Basic Quranic Terms* on which, according to him, revolves the whole axis of Islam and without which neither Islam can be strictly followed nor any invitation can be extended nor any work relating to establishment of Islam can be done. He also expressed the view, clearly and emphatically, that barring a limited period, these terms, as understood at the time of the descent of the Quran, assumed different meanings during the course of centuries so much so that bereft of their expanse and compass, they were applied in a very narrow and ambiguous sense as a result of which the real spirit of more than three-fourth of the Quran got obseure.

The way in which he interpreted and explained the terms and the emphasis he laid on them, being the core and focal points of the real spirit, led to a new type of exegesis of the Quran and Islam which had a political colouring and revolved round 'Kingdom of God' and 'Sovereignty of God' and the purpose of the revelation of the Quran and Islamic preachings was reduced to establishment of the Kingdom of God. The pattern he adopted in framing means and delineating the purpose and the new ideas and theories he evolved for worship and remembrance of God, can raise reasonable apprehension that the new generation, which would be influenced by such ideas and researches, and the party, which would be influenced by such literature, would not be mentally prepared to accept any other disposition and a new religious temper would be developed which will have nothing to do with the spirit that was generated by the company and guidance of the Holy Prophet (peace be on him), his efforts and injunctions and the efforts of his companions and which has been coming down uninterrupted through out the ages. It would amount to laying down a new track other than the one laid down by the Prophet, his companions, the *tabaeens* and their heirs.

This book discusses only this aspect of the problem. It has not been written in the manner of debate or disputation or in the language of law or judicial pronouncements. It expresses an apprehension and is a sincere effort based on the Quranic assertion that '*Din* is giving good counsel.' It has no organisational objective nor any political ambition.

Though there were persistent requests and strong impulses for fulfilling this obligation, and persistent enquiries, relating to the basic concepts of the Jamat and my opposition to them, were being made, I kept on postponing the task. The reason was that it was a very delicate job for the concepts were held by a party, its supporters, scholars with whom the author has friendly relations and for years had cooperated and collaborated with them in the field of Islamic invitation and the struggle for resolution of the problems facing the eommunity. Then again, that party has done great service in promoting intellectual awakening of Muslims who had received modern education and in restoring their confidence in the eternal value of their religion and its capacity to lead the world. The author had another apprehension that his criticism and assessment might be utilised by some quarters for political or party ends or they might be construed as motivated by personal ends which it is difficult to eschew without God's help.

Because of these considerations writing a book on such a subject was a difficult and unpleasant task. It might raise a volley of questions and lot of misgivings. To ascribe it to good intentions and to find justification for the critic or the author is difficult for many people. To decry it or to cast doubts and aspersions is much easier. One reason for this is that for a long time examples of detached criticism based on sincerity and justice and free from personal or political taints have been rare. Experience of people in this regard has been bitter and not many examples have been seen where people, rising above political or personal expediency and keeping religion and truth as the only criterion, have fearlessly endeavoured for establishment of the right and exposure of the false or where priority has been given to religion over personalities and movements, the founders of great powers and the leaders of *Din* and the community. That was the way of the Traditionists (*Muhaddisin*) and the Masters of critical examination and assessment in their treatment of great reformers, the pious and the righteous, rulers and conquerors of their ages.[1]

Another difficulty in the way of the author was that from the very beginning his way of penmanship and his approach to compilation or writing have been constructive, positive and uncontroversial and he always avoided controversial matters and

1. Examples of such upright and detached criticism can be seen in books like *Kitabul Majruhin* of Ibn Habban, *Meezanul Aitadal* of Zahabi and the preface of *Sahih Muslim*.

verbal disputations and wherever he was obliged to do so that was only a temporary and secondary affair[1] and he reverted again to his own approach and to meaningful discussions on principles and problems. It was no easy task for him to deviate from his life-long practice and chosen way[2].

However, against my personal inclination and attitude I decided to take up writing of this book when I had observed and fully realised that the literature which the party was bringing out was giving a new direction to the religious attitude and there was a great danger that a new meaning and interpretation of religion, and new set of values and new standards were likely to be evolved. There was a danger that the thinking and endeavour of the intelligent, educated, sincere, active and determined class were likely to leave the straight path of the Book and the *Sunnat*, the way of the Prophet, concern for the Hereafter, faith and accounting[3] and to deflect to the way of party organisation and to regain for the Muslims political power and governmental rule so much so that its return to the straight path may be difficult. God is aware that this unpleasant task has been done purely for upholding what is right and as an answer to various questions that had arisen.

1. As the author has done in some of his notes in his book *'Al-Nabuatu wal Anbiya fi Zu-al-Quran'*.
2. His book *Qadianism—A Critical Study* is a solitary exception which he has written about people outside the pale of Islam but claim to be Muslim.
3. According to many *ahadith*, acceptance and reward of not only many righteous deeds but also obligation are dependent upon their performance in faith, hope and belief though in the absence of faith their righteousness cannot be contemplated. This is explained by another *Hadith* of *Bukhari* that the deeds be done in the hope of reward and belief in the reward promised by God and desire for recompense and merit. This is the real spirit of deeds and it is to be strictly guarded.

It is hoped that the people belonging to the circle of Jamat-i-Islami will read this book closely and seriously and would not ascribe it to party prejudices or to serve any personal end or treat it as a measure of opposition to Islamic movement which is making strides that should gladden every believer in truth and any well-wisher of Islam.

Those who wish to serve religion sincerely and seriously and wish to see supremacy of Islam and the God's name and possess the spirit to search for the truth, proper religious understanding, its development and completion and their objective is truth and not any party or personality howsoever big, they have always welcomed healthy and constructive criticism, expression of different points of view and friendly suggestions. It is this unselfish criticism and objective assessment that has saved the *Ummat*, in the long journey of its history, thinking, interpretation and re-interpretation of Islamic laws and experiences, from fatal pitfalls and collective deviation and distortion. To stifle intellectual curiosity and evaluation and the search for knowledge would be a dangerous step for any party or school of thought. What the Arab poet of *Hamasa* said centuries back is still true—"In well-meaning complaints and reproach lies the secret of the life of parties and peoples". Constructive criticism has played a vital role in correction of opinions and thinking, in evaluation of theories and extension of juristic knowledge which have no parallel in the history of other religions and civilisations and they have ever been aids to the community in diverse circumstances and have smoothened its tasks. That way it saved the Ulama and thinkers from self-opinionatedness, attachment of too much value to themselves as being free from blemish and saved their followers from excessive exaggeration in their regard and helped to generate moderation and adherence to the right path which is a distinctive characteristic of Muslims, particularly of the *Ahle-Sunnat*.

When the door of scholarly and detached assessment was closed in other religions, particularly in Christianity, there were only few persons to do the courageous job, and they became victims to distortions by persons exceeding limits, the falsehood of the wicked and ridiculous explanations of the ignorant. As a result, on their soil grew up wild plants and bushes and dense forests which covered the face of the reality of the religion and its initial teachings. Therefore, the sacred *Shariat* has made enjoining of right and forbidding of wrong, necessary and binding aod stressed this course for every place and for every time and has treated indolence in this regard, and silence in the face of men of power and position, a major sin. It has treated expression of the right and just thing in the face of tyrannical powers as 'Superlative Jihad'. It is because of this that the common Muslims, and particularly the Ulama of Islam, have been discharging this obligation in adverse circumstances and against tyrannical and despotic rulers. Amir-ul-Mominin Hazrat Umar Farooq, whose might and awe shook the Caesars and Kasra (Qaiser), had given permission to every common and weak person to freely express his opinion. He had said, "If these people do not tell me the right thing, there is no merit in them and if I do not listen to their objections with grace, who would be worse than me."[1] He had once said, "A female said the right thing while a male made a mistake."[2]

There is no justification for keepling silence on the mistake, flaw, or forgetfulness of an esteemed person on the ground that he is the leader or is dedicated to the service or common good of

1. Imam Abu Yusuf; *Kitabul Khiraj* p. 7.
2. As reportad by Mohaddith Abdul Razzaq this refers to Hazrat Umar's statement' Do not be excessive in fixing *Mehr* of women'. A women referred him to the Quranic verse "If you have given her even a talent of gold, do not take back aught of it (Q. 4 : 20), whereupon Hazrat Umar said, 'A woman argued with him and won the point.' *Nil-al-Awtar*, vol. vi, p. 170).

the people which is benefitting Islam and Muslims or there is high expectation from him and pointing out his mistakes or giving him correct advice may promote lack of confidence in him or dissatisfaction. Well-meaning criticism and sound advice do not stand in the way of service of religion or crusading efforts nor impair any one's personal merits and attainments. Thus we see the companions pointing out his omission and forgetfulness to the leader of the prophets and the best of men (peace be on him). There is a Tradition that when in a *Salat* of four *rakats,* the Prophet said only two, the companion Zulyadayn asked him whether the prayer had been shortened or he did not say the remaining two in a moment of forgetfulness.[1] The Prophet did not take it ill nor censured any one, nor the companions drew any adverse inference from it. He and the companions took advantage of it and resaid the complete prayers.

In the same way Amirul Mominin Hazrat Umar, who had the highest conception of what was good for the community, deposed Saiyyidna Khalid, the Commander-in-Chief of the Muslim forces in the battle of Yarmuk, in the thick of the engagement and replaced him by Hazrat Abu Ubaida. If in the past the Muslims had not pointed out the mistakes and irregularities in the fear of creating discord in their ranks, the task of enjoining what is right and forbidding what is wrong, and the life giving current of upholding the truth, would have been cut off from collective morality and the life of the community and fresh blood would not have circulated in its veins. As a result the doubts and misgivings of the learned and the people of sound opinions and the concealment of many truths of religion would have been far more disastrous than the acknowledgment of any mistake of understanding or interpretation by any leader, Imam or the most distinguished litterateur. God alone is without any blemish and imperfection and apart from the sayings of His

1. *Tirmidhi* on the authority of Abu Huraira.

Apostle, people have a choice to accept or reject the view of others.

I am amazed that the party which was founded on independent and fearless criticism of many sectors of Islamic society and their movements and endeavours, should exhibit, on the part of its members and supporters, such hyper-sensitiveness against criticism or objections of others to their creating a halo of sanctity round the founder of the party.

Maulana Maududi has himself set up a pattern by writing in his book *A Short History of the Revivalist Movement in Islam* in which he has critically examined the contributions and attainments of well established revivalists of the *Din* and was not deterred from expressing his views about them isnpite of their greatness, and renown, and trust of the people in them and their affection and esteem for them.

The present book is a humble effort in the series started by Maulana Abul Ala Maududi. I may be excused when I say that there is no one-way traffic in scholarly criticism, search for the better and the sounder or in reflection and study. If one-way rule was to be applied in the world of thinking and writing, the intellect of man will despair, scholarly activity will be suspended, the zest for discovery of the better and the sounder will wither away which are like a blessed tree whose roots are firmly fixed in the ground, whose branches are touching the sky and which, by Grace of God, is yielding fruits at every moment.

What God says is true and He guides to the straight path.

S. Abul Hasan Ali Nadwi
Daira Shah Alam ullah, Rai Bareli

In the name of God, the most compassionate, the most merciful.

CHAPTER I

Meaning and Import of the Four Basic Terms of the Quran

THE eminent scholar and thinker of the day and the founder of Jamat-e-Islami, Maulana Saiyid Abul Ala Maududi, while mentioning the Quranic terms '*Ilah*', '*Rab*', '*Din*', and '*Ibadat*', and Islamic phraseology in his popular and famous book the *Four Basic Quranic Terms* wants to establish that at the time of the descent of the Quran, every addressee thereof whose mother tongue was Arabic, knew the import and meaning of the four basic Quranic terms. He writes,

> "When the Quran was first presented to the Arabs they all knew what was meant by *Ilah* or *Rabb* as both the words were already current in their language. They were not knew terms, nor were any new meanings put

upon them. They knew fully well what the connotations were and so, when it was said that Allah alone is the *Ilah*, and the *Rabb* and that no one has the least share in the qualities and attributes which the words denote they at once comprehended the full imoo rt, understood completely without any doubt or uncertainty as to what specifically was being declared to pertain to Allah exclusively and what was being hence denied to others. Those who opposed the precept were very clear in their minds as to the implications of denying others than Allah to be *Ilahs* or *Rabbs*, in any sense, while those who accepted it knew equally well what they would have to give up by their acceptance and what they would forego. Similarly, the words '*Ibadah*' and '*Din*' were in common use, and the people knew what was meant by '*Abd*', what state was implied by '*uboodiyyah*' (the state of being an '*abd*') what kind of conduct was referred to when the word '*ibadah*' was used, and what was the sense of the term '*Din*', so, when they were told to give up the *ibadah* of all others and reserve it exclusively for Allah, and give up all other *dins* and enter into the *Din* of Allah only, they felt no difficulty in concluding what the Quranic *d'awah* (message) implied and the drastic revolution in their way of life it sought to bring about".[1]

But according to him this state did not last long, these self-evident truths became obscure and the four fundamental terms of the Quran, which were accepted facts of Islam, got covered up by thick veils of ignorance, negligence and non-Arab influence. After writing the above mentioned paragraph he writes :

"But as centuries passed, the real meanings of these

1. S. Abul Ala Maududi, *Four Basic Quranic Terms.*, (Dalhi, 1980), pp. 5-6

terms gradually underwent subtle changes so that, in course of time, instead of the full connotations, they came to stand for only very limited meanings or restricted and rather vague concepts. One reason was the gradual decline of interest in the Arabic language and the other that the words ceased to have the same meaning for the later generations of Muslims that they had for the original Arabs to whom the Quran had been revealed. It is for these two reasons that in the more recent lexicons and commentaries many of the Quranic words began to be explained not by their original sense but by what they had by then come to stand for, e.g.,

> The word *Ilah*, as used in respect of others than God, came to be synonymous with idols or gods;
> The word *rabb* came to mean only someone who brings up or rears or feeds another or provides for his wordly needs;
> *'Ibadah* began to be understood as the performance of a set of rituals of "worship";
> *Deen* began to mean a religion, or belief in some precepts ; and
> The word *Taghoot* began to be translated to mean as idol or the Devil."[1]

Describing the consequence of this state of affairs, he writes, "This being the case, is it any wonder that, through the mist that has come to surround the precise sense of the four terms in question, more than three fourths of the teachings of the Quran, or rather, the real spirit there of, have become obscured and this is the main cause of the shortcomings that are to be seen in peoples' beliefs and acts despite the fact that they

1. *Four Basic Quranic Terms. op. cit.*, pp. 6-7

have not formally given up the faith of Islam but are still in its fold."[1]

Perspicacity of the Ummat and the Distinction of the Quran

On reading these passages one who has not made deep and extensive study and who is not aware of the fact that God has preserved this *Ummat* from going astray generally, can infer that the reality of the Quran remained hidden from the *Ummat* or the majority of it, for a long time and the *Ummat* remained collectively ignorant of the reality of the basic terms round which revolves the whole structure of the Book and on which rests the edifice of its teachings and exhortations and the veil could be lifted only by the middle of twentieth century.

On a cursory look this conclusion may not appear very damaging and serious but its impact on mind and the way of thinking would be far-reaching for it raises doubts in the capabilites of the *Ummat* which is not only the bearer of the religion and the message but is responsible for its expansion over the world and its elucidation and protection. It also casts doubts on the history of the *Ummat* and belittles the achievements of its renovators, reformers and religious doctors in scientific and scholarly fields and in their practices. For future also it will raise doubts about the authenticity of what is being said or understood today. It will also give strength to the philosophy of 'the apparent and the hidden' and 'the kernel and the shell' and make religious truths incomprehensible and obstruse riddles which was the way of different groups of Batinites in different times.

Relationship between Words and their Meanings.

Many of the readers who have not closely studied the

1. *Four Basic Quranic Terms*, *op. cit.*, p. 8

history of religions and schism may not be able to appreciate this brief statement. I am, therefore, reproducing what I have written in the first volume of my book the *Saviours of Islamic Spirit* about the technique of the Batinites.

> "The scripture has clearly laid down the tenets of belief and code of conduct, if only because these are meant to be understood and acted upon by every human being:
>
> > *And We never sent a messenger save with the language of his folk, that he might make (the message) clear for them.*
> >
> > (*Ibrahim* : 4)
>
> "The meaning of this verse is manifestly clear. The Prophet of Islam too had explained the import of divine revelations and lived up to those precepts so that his followers might not remain in any doubt. The vocabulary of the Quran and its meanings have thus been handed down, from the Prophet, without any break, and have ever afterwards been recognised and accepted by everyone as authentic and genuine, and to which no one raised any objection. The terms, Prophethood *(nabuwat)* and apostleship *(risalat)*, angels *(malaika)*, requital *(ma'ad)*, paradise *(jannat)*, hell *(dozakh)*, the law *(shariah)*, obligatory *(fardh)*, necessary *(wajib)*, lawful *(halal)*, unlawful *(haram)*, poor-due *(zakat)*, prayer *(salat)*, fast *(rozah)*, pilgrimage *(hajj)*, and similar other words convey a concise and definite purport of the doctrines, rites, ceremonies, and teachings of Islam. In truth and reality, these teachings and articles of faith have been handed down without any divergence whatsoever and so has been the vocabulary and terminology evolved to signify the former. The two have become so inter-dependent that one cannot

suffer any mutation without a variation in the other.

"Whenever the words 'Prophet', 'Apostle', 'Messenger', 'Prayer'or 'Poor-due' are used, these denote the same exposition as taught by the Prophet and understood by his companions and successors; all of whom acted upon these in a particualar manner and transmitted the import of these words which have been handed down by one generation to another. The Batinites knew that the interdependence of Quranic vocabulary and its meanings form the key to the exposition of the doctrines of Muslim faith; these constiute the moorings of intellectual and practical life of the *Ummah*, connecting the later generations with the fountainhead of divine guidance which lay in the past. If they could only drive a wedge between the past and the present, asunder the connecting link by rendering the import of Quranic vocabulary ambiguous and oracular, undefined and obscure, then the *Ummah*, could be made to give credence to any innovation or deviation, agnosticism or infidelity."[1]

The Basic Characteristics and Distinction of the Quran

Diversity between words and their meanings is against facts and the belief that the '*Din*' was not only given in book form but also transmitted in action from generation to generation and the transmission had included both words and their significance. God has described the Quran at numerous places as 'an open book' and a 'clear Arabic.'

At the start of chapter Joseph, God says, "*Alif. Lam.*

1. S. Abul Hasan Ali Nadwi, *Saviours of Islamic Spirit*, (Lucknow, 1976) Vol. I, pp. 106-107

Ra. These are the verses of the Book clear in itself." (Q. 12 : 1)

The *Surah* 'The Rock' starts as, "*Alif. Lam. Ra.* These are the verses of the scripture, a Quran, clear in itself." (Q. 15 : 1)

The chapter 'The Ant' begins as "*Ta. Sin.* These are the verses of the Quran—The Book lucid (in expression)". (Q. 27:1)

The first verse of the Chapter 'The Poets' is : "*Ta. Sin. Mim.* Here are the signs of the lucid Book!" (Q. 26 : 1)

In the chapter 'The Poets' is indication of the clarity and easy understanding of the Revelation—

"Verily this hath descended from the Lord of all domains of existence. The Trusted Spirit hath let it descend upon thy heart, that thou mayest function as a warner, through the medium of the clear Arabic tongue." (Q. 26 : 192-193)

The chapter "The smoke' starts as "*Ha. Mim.* By the clear Book." (Q. 44 : 1)

The Quran has repeatedly and emphatically stressed that it is a clear, lucid, explicit and a book easy to understand Then how can it be believed that the Book could not convey the real import and significance of the four basic terms round which, it is said, revolves the entire gamut of beliefs, action, exhortations and preachings[1].

1. In his commentary on "*Al-Mubin*" in *Surah* 'The Rock' Maulana Maududi writes 'it means that these are the the verses of the Quran which clearly explain its meaning and purpose.'

At many places in the Quran it has been said that its verses are firm, distinct and lucid. Says it,

> "He it is Who has sent down to them the Book: Some verses of it are definite in meaning. These form the mother of the Book (the basic therein)."

> "And the believers say, 'why does not a revelation come down (to declare war against them who do not believe).' But when a decisive revelation is sent down, giving therein the order to fight, thou seest the diseased of the heart look towards thee with the look of one who is sinking at the hour of death." (Q. 47 : 20)

> "Here is a Book whose verses are complete in their form and content and are set forth clearly by one who is All-wise and All-informed." (Q. 11 : 1)

The eminent exegesist Hafiz Ibn Katheer in explaining the verse 'Definite forming the mother of the Book' writes that 'it is so clear and explicit in logic that none can bear any doubts about them'. He quotes Muhammad bin Yasar about them, 'They are the assertion of God, support of His servants and serve to silence the opponents and the critics. Their real meaning cannot be twisted or distorted.'[1]

Allama Alusi in his famous commentary, '*Ruh-ul-Ma'ani*' explains '*Muhakamat*, as follows, "Definitive is a quality of the verses meaning thereby that the verses in their meaning are explicit, obvious in their logic, definite in their language and unassailable by any doubt or apperhension."[2]

1. *Tafsir Ibn Katheer*, Vol. I, commentary on the chapter Family of Imran.
2. *Tafsir Ruh-ul-Ma'ani*, Vol. I, Surah Family of Imran

As regards the Quran being plain and distinct *(Mufassal)* there is mention about it at fifteen places.[1]

These qualities and definitions negative the contention that many basic truths of the Quran remained concealed for a long time. In the chapter 'The Rock' God has said "Without doubt, it is We Who have sent down this guidance, and without doubt, We shall guard it." (Q. 15 : 9)

The announcement and the promise of protection implies appreciation of the meaning and purpose of the scripture, its implementation and adoption in life. What can be the value or importance of a book and what can be the benefit and outcome of its protection if, for a long time, it remains in abeyance, un-understood and un-acted upon? But God had addressed the Prophet, "For collection (of its various parts) and its recitation (in a form) rests with Us. When We deliver, you are to listen and recite in the same manner. It is Our responsibility to let its meaning be clear." (Q. 75 : 17-19)

In explaining 'letting its meaning be clear' Hakim-ul-Islam Shah Wali Ullah Dehlavi writes in his masterpiece *'Izalat -ul-Khifa*:

> " God says that explanation of the Quran is His responsibility and that in every age He would raise a considerable body of persons who would explain the meaning, elucidate the words and the reasons and occasions for descent of its various parts so that the true import and significance may be manifest to the people. This comes later to its memorisation and preaching. The Holy Prophet

1. The Cattle, 58, 97, 98, 126 : The Heights, 32, 52, 174 ; the Repentance, 11 ; Jonah, 5, 24 ; the Romans, 28 ; the Thunder, 2; Hud, 1; Fussilat, 3, 44.

was himself its commentator and elucidator. Writing of exegesis followed its collection in a standard form and the general practice of its recitation. This started with Hazrat Ibn Abbas".[1]

The supposition that such basic words, without which the purpose, significance and meaning of the Quran and its commandments and exhortations cannot be understood, remained undiscerned and obscure for centuries would be against the Divine promise of clarification contained in the words 'would let its meaning be clear.'

Did the Community as a whole ever Fall in Error,

The type of research conducted and the style of description adopted by Maulana Maududi would lead one to conclude that the *Ummat* went through a long period of ignorance of the true import of the basic terms and their connotations and a mystery on which depended the soundness of their thinking and action. That would be tantamount to clear ignorance and negligence and even to perdition. But the Quran, the *Sunnat*, the compilations of *Ahadith*, collectively establish that, unlike previous communities, this community would never fall in general and universal error. Many eminent Muhaddithin and Ulama have held that though the famous Tradition 'My community would never collectively fall in error and deviation', is not established in so many words, the import of the Tradition is, nevertheless, true. The famous Andulasian Muhaddith and critic Allama Abu Muhammad Ali bin Hazm (d. 456 A. H.) has written in his book, *'Al-Ihkam fil Usul-il-Ihkam'*—

"The Muhaddithin say that it is true that the *Ummat-e-Muhammadiya* shall never agree on something false for the Prophet (peace be on him) himself had said that in

1. *Izalatul Khifa*, p. 51

every age there would be torch bearers of the truth. It is narrated that the Prophet (peace be on him) had said, "My community would never collectively fall in error and deviation". Though its words and authenticity of transmission are not fully established, yet its import and consequence are proved by many fully established *ahadith* which prophecy the presence in every age of upholders of truth"[1].

Hafiz Ibn Qaiyyim says "We are beholden to God that the community collectively would never agree to give up even one *Sunnat* except what had been rescinded by the Prophet himself."[2]

Hafiz Ibn Katheer writes in his famous commentary on the verse of the chapter, 'Women', "As for him who sets himself against the Apostle despite the opening out for him the right path and follows any path other than that of the faithful....." (Q. 4 : 115) says, "A guarantee has been given to this *Ummat* that it has been safeguarded from agreeing upon any thing wrong."[3]

Shaikhul Islam Ibn Taimiya writes about consensus, "The consensus of the community is always right for, praise be to God, it can never agree on error or falsity. This distinction has been spelled out in the Book and the *Sunnat*. The Quran says, "You are the best of communities .... who shall follow the Apostle, the Ummi Prophet, whose advent is foretold in the Torah and the Evangel. He will enjoin them what is right and forbid them what is wrong" and "The faithful men

1. This is the view of Allama Ibn Hazm but the famous Muhaddith and critic, Allama Sakhawi says that it [is such a *Hadith* that its text is well-known, its authorities are many and its proof plentiful.(Al-Ihkam, Vol. iv, p. 131)
2. *Aylam al-Muwaqqayin*, Vol. II, p. 320
3. *Tafsir Ibn Katheer*, Vol. II, p. 393

and women, are friends of one to the other, they enjoin what is good and forbid what is evil." If the community were to adopt erroneous ways, it would mean that the obligation of enjoining what is right and forbidding what is wrong, has not been discharged even though the Quran says, "And likewise, have We moulded you into a model society that you might be a pattern unto others, even as the Prophet has been a pattern unto you."[1] (Q. 2 : 143)

The Dictate of Intelligence

Ordinary intelligence cannot accept the supposition that this great community in which were born very outstanding and eminent Ulama, scholars, litterateurs and savants in every age, was continuously ignorant of the basic truths on which depend the understanding and preaching of the Quran, particularly in proximity to the prophetic era. Even Maulana Maududi does not accept that the community erred in understanding any *Hadith* or decisive verse of the Quran what to say of the basic truths, and the error could continue for any length of time. In discussing the famous *Hadith* 'Imams from amongst the Quraish,' he writes, "can it ever be accepted that the Ulama of the community failed collectively to understand a definite statement and continued to remain in error for centuries"[2], even though this *Hadith* has nothing to do with beliefs, or necessities of life or requirements of the religion.

On the same principle, the Maulana has based his arguments against Qadiainis in interpreting the words 'the last of the prophets' which has been understood down the ages in only one sense and the community has been all along quoting the interpretation of its stalwarts and pillars.[3]

1. *Fatawah Shaikhul Islam Ahmad ibn Taimiya*, Vol. XIX, pp. 176-177
2. *Tafhimat* Vol. III, p. 176, New Delhi Edition.
3. Maulana Maududi : *Tafhimul Quran*. Commentary on Surah Ahzab.

Comments of a distinguished Egyptian scholar and the Leader of Ikhwan.

Allama Hasan Ismail al-Huzaibi, who was selected as the leader of Ikhwan-al-Muslimin, after Imam Shahid Hasan al-Banna, and on whose profundity, erudition, sincerety, perspicacity and steadiness, the community was justly proud, comments on the theory of Maulana Maududi regarding the four basic terms in his Book '*Dawatun la-Quzat*' as follows: "The assertion is factually and historically incorrect for whatever meaning might have been given to them in the days of ignorance, the Quran fixed their meanings and import and explained fully and clearly each of these terms. Their significance is unveiled in such a manner that it leaves not an iota of doubt or ambiguity. This exposition has left no necessity for search for their literal or dictionary meanings or what was understood by the terms before the descent of the Quran. No Muslim can have the slightest doubt that the manner of presentation of the Quran, its exposition and elucidation are not decisive, lucid, authoritative and of the highest standard. Not only this but it is imperative to adopt and rely upon and to accept their demand and consequence, irrespective of the fact whether they correspond with what was understood by them in pre-Islamic days or is contradictory to those concepts.'[1]

Then he proceeds to give examples[2] from the Quranic verses where they have been used: "Will it be true to say that when the Arabs were divided into clans and tribes and each had its own dialect, when there was no common government, no common beliefs, culture and civilization, when they were illiterate and there were only a handful who had any thing to do with reading or writing, when they were enveloped in the

1. *Dawatun la-Quzat*, pp. 19-20
2. *Ibid*, p.p. 20-25

gloom of ignorance and decadence, when they had among them no divine book, nor any scholarly tradition, when they were so low and inferior, then the correct significance and import of the terms *'Ilah'*, *'Rab'*, *'Ibadat'* and *'Din'* were commonly known to them and so well publicised that every person knew them equaly well without any doubt or ambiguity, but when God sent down His Scripture with the verse, "without doubt, it is We Who have sent down this Revelation, and without doubt We shall guard it" and which is preserved from any interpolation or tampering as the Quran says, "Falsehood shall not touch it whether it cometh either from in front of it or from behind it" (Q. 41 : 42), and in the text of which there is no ambiguity nor is there any flaw in its exposition and by the daily recitation of which millions of servants of God attain His pleasure and nearness and the verses of which are loudly recited in congregational prayers, then the meaning and significance of the terms receded behind a curtain and they were no longer current and well known and the *Ummat* lost the bounty vouchsafed to it. Is it becoming for any man to make such a fantastic assertion when the Book of God is preserved in the hearts of Muslims and otherwise. If any body reads only *Surah Fatiha* and *Surah Ikhlas* or the *Surah al-Falak* and *An-Nas*, on him will be manifest the meaning and significance of these terms of which the pre-Islamic people had not even an inkling. The assertion of the author (Maulana Maududi) that in Muslim society the terms *'Ilah'*, *'Rabb'* *'Din'* and *'Ibadat'* were not understood as they were understood in pre-Islamic days at the time of descent of the Quran, is an unwarranted and untrue assertion and a baseless and fatuous accusation. The few verses of the Quran that I have cited as an example alone establish the meaning of Divinity and Providence. In no age the commentators of the Quran rested with one explanation of the word *'Rab'*, but explained it at every place in the context of the verse[1]. (So wide and deep is the range and character of the term)."[2]

Allama Hasan Ismail al-Huzaibi then proceeds to quote various verses of the Quran to explain the range of meaning of the term *'Rab'* and then elaborates the meaning of the term *'Ibadat'* and *'Din'* in the light of Quranic veses. He then reproduces the statement of Maulana Maududi that "When the Quran was first presented to the Arabs they all knew what was meant by *'Ilah'* or *'Rab'* as the words were already current in their language. They were not new terms, nor were any new meanings put upon them. They knew fully well what the connotations were and so, when it was said to them that Allah alone is *'Ilah'* and *'Rab'* and that no one else has the least share in the qualities and attributes which the words denote, they atonce comprehanded the full import, understood completely without any doubt or uncertainty as to what was being declared to pertain to Allah exclusively and what was denied to others" and comments, "if this discourse is intended to assert that at the time of conferment of apostleship (on the Holy Prophet), every Arab in Najd and Hijaz had fully understood his preachings, the reality of *'Tauhid'* and had grasped the full implication of the first testimony that 'there is no god but God' ,the assertion will have to be substantiated by proof and it would not be just enough to say that the meaning of *'Ilah'* and *'Rab'* were well known and current among the Arabic speaking people. Who can say that he had carried out any census and knew the state of every individual when all the people of Najd and Hejaz etc., did not even

1. *Dawatun la-Quzat*, p 25. The fact is that in every age this term was understood and correctly explained but the term was not confined to one particular meaning or aspect — the author.
2. Translator.

belong to the Arabian race having Arabic as their mother tongue, when a great number of outsiders had settled down there, when amongst them were a large number of slaves brought from different countries and races and many were free foreigners having non-Arabic languages of their own. History has preserved the names of many companions belonging to Iranian, Roman and Abysinnian races and the Quran has indicated their presence in the verse, 'And indeed We know that they say, without doubt a human being teacheth him. But the speech of the person they hint at is non-Arabic while this is clearly the Arabic language."[1] (Q. 16: 103)

***

1. *Dawatun la-Quzat*, p. 30

CHAPTER II

Maligning the World of Islam

WHEN Maulana Maududi, unhesitatingly, expresses the view that in later centuries the four basic terms were not understood in the sense they were understood at the time of the descent of the Quran and they got so heavily cloaked that not only three-fourth preachings of the Quran, but its real spirit was lost to view, it would mean naturally that to him the whole past history of the *Ummat* presents a spectre of unchecked decline and continuous decadence and the history of the middle period appears to him a barren desert and wilderness (though he has acknowledged the deeds of many revivalists working in a limited sphere in that period) and in this immense darkness, there were, according to him, only occasional flashes in some corners of the world of Islam of the lightning of religious endeavour and reform—something akin to the Quranic verse, "The lightning well-nigh snatcheth away their sight, whenever it flasheth, they walk into its light and whenever darkness closeth upon them, they hold back". (Q. 2 : 20)

The logical result of such a trend of thinking and presumptions would be that probably excluding the period of the companions and the *Taba'een*,[1] a sensitive and educated young Muslim who is not conversant with the vast history of Islam's intellectual and reformative endeavours, would begin to doubt the eternal character of Islamic preachings, Islam's capacity of producing men of calibre, the freshness and fruit-bearing capacity of the Islamic tree, his conviction would be eroded and he would become a victim of despondency and disillusion, of doubt and uncertainty. He can imagine that even after watering the soil of the wilderness cannot become fertile.

Some readers might start thinking that we are not being just and fair to Maulana Maududi for all Muslim reformers had started their reformative movement with criticism of and expression of dissatisaction with the Muslim society of the day. For instance, Imam Ghazali in his book *Ihya-ul-Uloom*, Allama Ibn Taimiya in his books *ar-Rad alal Bakari* and *ar-Rad alal Akhnaiy*, Hazrat Shaikh Abdul Qadir Jilani in his scintillating sermons and addresses and Shah Waliullah Dehlavi and his brilliant grandson Maulana Ismail Shaheed in their treatises, had adopted a severe critical approach. But it should not be forgotten that these dignitaries had confined their criticism to the aberrations and waywardness of the society of the day and had not painted a lurid picture of the entire Islamic history and all the periods and domains of the Islamic *Ummat*. It is one thing to criticise the society of the day in order to reform and re-invigorate it and another to malign the whole history of the *Ummat*. There is a world of difference in the two sets of approaches.

If anybody writes in a fashion that leads to un-warranted conclusion that the Islamic record is dark and barren, that the *Ummat-e-Muhammadiyya* does not possess creative ability and

1. His writings go to indicate that even that period was not totally exemplary and ideal.

nothing but darkness, deviation and apostasy prevailed in Islamic history, it will have to be inferred that the writer has jumped to fatuous conclusion, and his knowledge of the history of reform and renovation in woefully incomplete. The writer himself committed this type of mistake in some of his earliest writings undertaken before he had acquired maturity of thought and had not made extensive study and specialised research.[1] The writer had realised his mistake and when he wrote his more famous book *Islam and the World* he added the following paragraph under the heading Revival and Restoration.

> "So far, however, as the basic values of religion were concerned, they remained intact and free from all distortion. They remained absolutely free from all kinds of innovation, interpolation, mis-construction or suppression. Islam did never wink at the lapses of its followers. It was always on the alert, correcting, mending, admonishing; the Quran and the Sunnah were continually there intact and unpolluted—to guide and to judge on occasions of doubt and dispute. They kept alive the spirit of defiance against the libertinism of the ruling classes and against the other un-Islamic influences. The whole course of Islamic history is lighted up with the crusading endeavours of conscious, determined, brave-hearted men who, like the true successors of the Prophet, faced the challenge of the time and restored, revived and kept on moving the *Millat* by resorting to *Jihad* and *Ijtihad*. These two principles, which embody the dynamism of Islam, could never suffer a vacuum in its structure. They remained operative ceaselessly in the body of Islam as living

1. As happened in the author's famous and largely published book *Seerat Saiyid Ahmad Shaheed*' when this impression was given under the caption of the 'Saiyid's Times.'. This was the author's first book written at the age of twenty-two.

factors, holding aloft the torch of religious endeavour in the midst of the severest tempests. Thus it was that darkness was never allowed to spread itself over the whole world of Islam."[1]

I had further added that:

"With all their failings, the Muslims were nearer to the path of the prophets than any other people. For this reason, whatever of their former power and prestige was left, continued to serve as a deterrent to ignorance. They were still a force in the world, commanding respect from far and near. But, internally, they had been shrivelling and declining. This fact could not be concealed for long from the outside world. The fiction of their strength was finally broken towards the middle of the 13th century, when they were attacked by wave after wave of the savage nations and hostile powers and Islamic lands fell into the hands of their enemies."[2]

For retracting tbe conclusions drawn up in haste by the author in his first work, he wrote the four volumes of his book the *Saviours of Islamic Spirit* in which he has extensively portrayed the intellectual and religious efforts of Islam, its social history and revivalist and reformative endeavours and has introduced in a copious way the leaders of such movements and has categorically stated in the Introduction to the book that in Islam there has been a continuity of reformative movements and there were no long interregnums of suspense or inaction.

Maulana Maududi in writing a critical chapter on the history of the community adopts a forceful style in a rheto-

1. S. Abul Hasan Ali Nadwi, *Islam and the World*, (Luckonw 1973), pp. 96:
2. *Ibid.*, pp. 100

rical and exciting strain quite distinguishable from his well-known style of writing. He writes, "For nearly three centuries the spirit of the Muslims exhibited itself in its fullness for research, interpretation and re-interpretation for independent appreciation and enquiry and unshackled search for the truth which the holy Prophet (peace be on him) had engendered in his followers. But after that the oppression of the rich, the rulers and the Ulama and Mashaikhs began to erode that spirit. The right of the thinkers to think, the right of eyes to see, the right of the tongues to speak were denied and usurped. Right from the courts to madrsas and Khanqahs Muslims were trained in a slavish mentality The slavery of the spirit and the body was imposed upon them. The rulers of the courts instilled slavish mentality by prescribing bowing and prostration before them, the educationists of the madrsas injected the venom of worshipping of great men besides the worship of God, the Khanqah people placed the yoke of sacred slavery, heavier than which man had never before invented, on the necks of people by distorting the prophetic way of taking fealty *(Bait)*. When heads can bow down upto the ground, before things other than God, when hands can remain folded in the posture of *Namaz* before other than God, when to lift up one's eyes before another man becomes a gesture of disrespect, when hands and feet of men begin to be kissed, when man becomes the lord and master of man and his sustainer, when man exercises his own volition in the matter of the enjoined and forbidden, when he arrogates to himself independence from the Book and the *Sunnat*, when man is taken as free from fault and blemish, when the ordinances of men and their opinions are treated as compulsory for obedience, may be not in the realm of belief but in actual practice, in the same way as God's ordinances, then take it that people have greatly digressed from the dictum that is contained in the Quranic verse "We serve God only and associate nothing with Him and that none of us shall take another for his Lord to the exclusion of God", (Q. 3 : 64). After this no literary and scholarly, ethical or spiritual progress is possible. Decline and decadence are bound to be its result.[1]"

In reviewing the work and services of the great revivalists of Islam in his book, entitled *A Short History of the Revivalist Movement in Islam* the Maulana has gone to the extent of saying, "History reveals that the ideal *Mujaddid* is yet to born. Caliph 'Umar bin 'Abdul 'Aziz might have attained this position but he did not get a chance to achieve it. All the *Mujaddids* who appeared after him accomplished work in one particular or the other aspect only but none achieved the distinction of becoming the ideal *Mujaddid*.[2]"

1. *Tafhimat* Vol. I, pp, 137, published by Central Maktaba-e-Jamat-e-Islami, New Delhi
2. S. Abul Ala Maududi, *A Short History of the Revivalist Movement in Islam*, (Lahore, 1963), p. 38

CHAPTER III

Continuous Efforts for Supremacy of the Truth

TO draw such a conclusion from history and this way of thinking are opposed to the text and the spirit of clear *Ahadith* which foretell that there will not be a moment in the life of the community which would be bereft of the presence of upholders of the truth nor their endeavours in this direction will cease. Bukhari and Muslim record—

"Some people of my community will always be supreme and exalted and their success and dominance will continue till the Doomsday"[1]

Tirmidhi records—

"A group in my community will always be successful and those who will not support them can put them to no loss and this will go on till the end of the world."[2]

1. *Bukhari; Sahih, Kitab al-Manaqib.*
2. *Jame Tirmidhi. Kitab al-fitan.*

The Tradition quoted by Ibn Maja is still more precise—

"A group in my community will always be actively engaged in matters of religion and circulation of the orders of God and their opponents can in no way thwart them."[1]

Tirmidhi has yet another *Hadith* to report—

"My community is like rains and no one can say about rains whether its beginning or the last part is more beneficial."[2]

Ḥakim has reported in the *Mustadrak*—

"A group in my community will always be successful and victorious in the matter of truth till the end of the world."[3]

Continuity of Endeavour for Reform and Revival.

An unbiased, wide and deep study of history, not limited to commonly known and imitative books and current publications, contradicts the view of Maulana Maududi and establishes without any doubt that efforts for reform and revival, struggle against spurious movements and turmoil of the times, internal and external assaults on Islam, and conspiracies of its enemies, conceptual and intellectual waywardness against ethical values and actual deflections and improprieties, confrontation with them and presentation of Islam in its pristine purity had continued uninterrupted throughout the ages. If any painstaking and determined student of the history of Muslims makes serious study and asserts with all sense of responsibility that every link of this golden chain is linked with another and no link is missing, the statement cannot be ascribed to wishful thinking or any motive to give intellectual deception to the community. This

1. *Ibn Maja ; Sunnan, Kitab al-fitan.*
2. *Tirmidhi ; Jame.*
3. Hakim, *Mustadrak*

is not the fault of history of Islam but of the historians in the presentation.[1] If on any subject well-compiled historical document is not available, it does not deny the facts, nor the presence of material and historical evidence. This is an experience frequently met in scholarly and academic research and study of history. In the language of logic and metaphysics, slightly different from that of history, Shaikh-ul-Islam Ibn Taimiya drew attention to a truth when he said, "Absence of knowledge does not necessarily imply absence of existence of something." If any learned man had not the opportunity, in his particular circumstances and engagements or as a result of his own inclination, to make a detailed study of this subject, it does not argue that reformative and revivalist efforts were never made.

Negative Thinking and Approach

Attempts to denigrate the capability of the community to produce profound men, the fruit-bearing capacity of the Islamic tree verified by the Quran as, "yielding fruits at all moments by the will of God" (Q. 14: 25), to look askance at revivalist and revolutionary endeavours in its long history or to belittle them or to view them with coloured spectacles have been the technique and strategy of misguided sects and groups or anarchic elements calculated to build up their own edifice on the ruins of Islamic history and Islamic thinking. They believe that unless they create dissatisfaction over the historical mass and contempt towards it, their own 'innovation and research' will not gain value and proper climate would not be created for the success of their own movements. In this connection many movements and group leaders can be named but I could never imagine that Maulana Maududi could evolve such a technique in a planned manner. His intentions may be above board but the natural consequence of this type of presentation is inevitable. Those who content

1. The author's book *Saviours of Islamic Spirit*, Vols. 1 to 111, will amply bear out this assertion.

themselves with study of his writings and who have understood Islam, its preachings and history solely from his articles and writings, they are so disappointed with the outcome of Islamic thinking and action, with the exception of the first one-third part of its past, that Halis' couplet can well apply to them,

> I have seen the poetry (works) of every one,
> Do not make me comment, for manners stand in the way.

CHAPTER IV

Sovereignty of 'Ilah and Rab'

ACCORDING to Maulana Maududi even among the four basic terms of the Quran, the pivotal role is played by the sovereignty of *Ilah* and *Rab* and *Din* and *Ibadat* are designed to draw people to this focal point. Explaining *Ilah* he writes "We can, therefore, safely conclude that the essence of godhood is authority, whether it is conceived as sovereignty of a supernatural kind over the whole universe, or on the basis that man is bound by God's law in his wordly life and that all of His injunctions are to be complied with because they emante from Him."[1]

He proceeds to say, "It will be seen that there is one central idea running through all these verses, and that is that Godhood and authority are inextricably interconnected and are, in essence and significance, one and the same thing. He who has no authority can be no god, and it is but fitting that he should not be so. And He Who has all due authority, He alone can

1 S. Abul Ala Maududi, *Four Basic Quranic Terms*, p. 20

be, and ought to be, God because all the needs which one might refer to a god, or the experiencing of which might turn one's thoughts to someone supposedly gifted with divinity can only be fulfilled if the person or being involved has in fact the power and the authority to be able to meet them. Hence, we must conclude that it is meaningless to regard anyone without the necessary power and authority to have any part of godhood: it is absolutely contrary to reason and reality, and it is quite absurd as well as useless to turn to these for help.[1]"

In explaining *'Rab'* and *'Rabubiyat'* he writes :

> "The foregoing verses bring out as clearly as possible that the Holy Quran uses *Rabubiyat* as exactly synonymous with sovereignty."[2]

Categorically he says that the real definition of *'Rab'* is Supreme Authority and *'Ibadat'* and servitude is obedience and loyalty to this Supreme Authority. A prophet is representative of the Supreme Authority and it is by that token that he has to be obeyed. Man is only a subject of the Supreme Power and his loyalty and worship should be reserved for Him. In commenting upon the verse of Family of Imran and the teaching of Hazrat Eisah (Jesus), "Verily God is my Lord and your Lord, so serve Him. This is the straight path" (Q. 3:51), he has adopted a purely political language and interpretation. He says :

"This shows that like other prophets, Jesus had also based his teachings on the following three fundamentals :

(1) The Supreme Authority to which mankind should submit and surrender exclusively belongs to Allah and all

1.S. Abul Ala Maududi. *Four Basic Quranic Terms*, pp. 24-25

2. *Ibid.*, p. 76

the social and moral systems should be built entirely on it;

(2) Being a representative of the same Paramount Power, a Prophet must be obeyed unconditionally;

(3) Allah alone is entitled to prescribe laws and regulations for making things lawful or unlawful, pure or impure; consequently all laws imposed by others must be abolished.

"Thus it is clear that Jesus, Moses, Muhammad and all other Prophets (Allah's peace be upon them all) had one and the same mission. Those people who aver that different Prophets were sent with different missions and to fulfil different aims, are gravely mistaken. Anyone, who is delegated by the Absolute Master of the Universe to His subjects, cannot have any other mission than to prevent the people from becoming disobedient to and independent of Him, and to forbid them to set others to rank with Allah as partners in His Authority in any way. For, they are sent to invite the people to surrender and submit and be loyal to the Almighty God and worship Him alone."[1]

Dilating upon the extent and unity of power and authority he tries to prove that there is no difference between polytheism *(shirk)* and considering any one's orders as binding for obedience. He writes, "All are different facets of a single, autocratic authority and sovereignty which is absolutely indivisible. If anyone regards the word of someone else to be deserving of obedience without any sanction from God, he is as much guilty of the offence of *Shirk* as the one who prays to or worships someone other than God. And if someone regards himself as the lord and

1. S. Abdul Ala Maududi; *The Meaning of the Quran*, Vol. II, (Delhi-1973) p. 236 (n. 48).

master and absolute monarch of any part of earth in the political sense, this act too amounts as much to a claim to godhood as it would if he were to tell people that he was their helper and patron and guardian in the supernatural sense. That is why the Qur'an emphasises, wherever it speaks of creation or of the destinies of creatures or the mangement of the universe, that:

> To Him belongs the ultimate dispensation of men's affairs (and of other things in creation too)—His is the kingdom——
>
> There is no sharer in His Suzerainty—

All of which clearly shows that godhood includes monarchy and rulership: And it is also stressed that *Tawheed* necessarily requires that in this sense too no one should be believed to have any share with God."[1]

Similarity in views of Saiyid Qutb and Maulana Maududi

Saiyid Qutb Shaheed, a dear and learned friend of the author and a renowned writer of Egypt, was deeply impressed by Maulana Maududi's book *The Four Basic Quranic Terms* and was in total agreement with him. He describers sovereignty as a speciality of divinity and he does not too strongly condemn the idol worshipping of the day of ignorance or worship of other than God. To him it was just a primitive and simple form of worship of the ancient days of ignorance. In his famous book '*Ma'alimu fit-Tareeq*' he writes, "The modern ignorance rests on the encroachment of people on God's domain of sovereignty and authority. By granting it to some men it accepts them as their '*Rab*' and this is not done in the primitive and

1. S. Abdul Ala Maududi, *Four Basic Quranic Terms*, (Delhi—1980), pp. 28—29

simple way as was the custom of the ancient days of ignorance. On the contrary, it claims that man has a perfect right to form theories and values, to lay down laws and regulations and systems and to enunciate political philosophy as distinct from God's system of governance and in contradication to His will."[1] He equates worship *(Ibadat)* with the action of men to take men as their master and to follow the rules framed by them. He goes on to say, "In short, besides the Islamic system, in every system man worships man in one form or the other and in Islamic system and only in Islamic system men are totally free from worship of other men and they treat God as the sole object of worship, follow His ordinances and injunctions and bow down before Him."[2]

He then proceeds to describe the Arabs to whom the Quran was first addressed, "In the view of an Arab conversant with the real meaning and significance of Arabic words, '*La Ilah-il-lallah*' means that sovereignty is for God alone and only His *Shariat* is to be followed and none else has any sovereign rights over others for that is the exclusive right of God."[3] He treats reservation of sovereignty for God alone as the real import of '*La-ilaha illallah*'. He thinks it necessary to teach real Islam to Muslims who just claim to be Muslims or whose names find place as such in registers of birth. He writes, "They have to be told that firstly Islam means believing, in its real meaning, the concept of '*La-illaha illallah*' i.e., acknowledgement of overlordship of God alone in every matter and rejection of those who make any encroachment upon it and claim authority."[4]

At one place he writes, "The declaration of exclusive *Rabubiyet* of God means total revolt, revoluion and rising in every

1. *Ma'alimu fit-Tariq*, p.8
2. *Ibid*, p. 8
3. *Ibid* p. 25
2. *Ibid.*, p. 35

corner of the globe against the authority of man (or in other words his divinity) which may appear in any form, shape, system or philosophy."[1]

To treat rulership as the central point and speciality of divinity and *Rabubiyat* will logically mean that to accept and follow any man-made laws in any matter is to negate religion and to ascribe partners in sovereignty of God which in the view of these gentlemen is nothing short of ascribing partners in divinity and providence.

Saiyid Qutub in his commentany *Fi-Zilal al-Quran* on the verse '*This is the eternal religion*' in chapter Joseph says,

> "This alone is the eternal religion. And so long as people do not follow God alone and recognise only His sovereignty religion has no meaning nor the worship of God has any value. If in any matter they follow other than God their subordination to God is imperfect and un-reliable for the unity of Divinity calls for unity of Providence *(Rabubiyat)* and there are only two external manifestation of *Rabubiyat*, viz., God's sovereignty and His worship. In this way both the words have the same connotation and are co-related. The worship that will distinguish a Muslim from a non-Muslim will be complete obedience and servility to the sovereignty of God."[2]

From this he draws the conclusion, "This definition of '*Din*' is a self-evident and a certain truth. If any one acknowledges the greatness of other than God and in any matter of life obeys him, he is neither a Muslim nor has he anything to do with religion. But one who believes in the sovereignty of God and

1. *Ma'alimu fit-Tariq*, p.59
2. *Fi-Zilal al-Quran*, Vol. 12. p. 200

is not prepared to follow any creature of God, nor bows before him, he is a Muslim and in the fold of the religion."[1]

Exaggeration and its contradiction.

It appears that in Egypt some people had so much exceeded the limits in advocating this theory, in its details and application, that Allama Huzaibi considered it necessary to contradict it. In his book, referred to before '*Duwatun La-Quzat*', after reproducing the view of Maulana Maududi on sovereignty of God, he writes, "Some people mistakenly believe that in the view of Maulana Maududi it is impossible that God should permit men to devise for themselves administrative arrangements or laws that may regulate or systematize any sphere of their lives".[2] Considering this as an unimaginable proposition, he writes, "The fact is that God has given volition to us in many matters so that in the light of our intelligence and for the common good of people and within the limits God has fixed, and for which He has given us ability, we may regulate in a manner that we do not make what is lawful, unlawful and vice versa".[3] He says, "There are three ingredients of *Shariat*—the obligatory, the forbidden, and the permissible. What the *Shariat* has declared lawful and forbidden will remain so till the Doomsday but so far as permissibles are concerned, Muslims are authorised to regulate what is required to be regulated for the common necessity and common good as established by clear verses of the Quran. In this category fall the Shura laws (i.e., those made by men by mutual consulation and deliberation) which derive their authority from the Quranic verse "their affairs are regulated by mutual consultation." The traffic control rules, rules governing health and sanitation, regulations pertaining to prevention of damage to crops and agriculture,

1. *Ma'alimu fit-Tariq* p.200
2. *Duwatun La Quzat*,p.72
3 *Ibid.* p.73

rules pertaining to irrigation system, the educational code, rules for organisation and management of trade and industry, administative rules, rules relating to armed forces, planning of cities, building regulations prescribed by the governments or civic authorities, all fall in this category. The guiding principles and the reasons and objects of these rules derive sanction from *Sunnat* and the practice of the companions."[1] He then categorically states, "This exposes the falsity of the theory that framing of laws, in whatever petty matters, is the exclusive attribute and function of God and whosoever frames laws arrogates to himself the attribute and authority of God and stakes a claim for equality with Him or revolts against Him."[2]

It appears that things had gone to this ridiculous extreme that some people started thinking that those who accept man-made laws are outside the pale of Islam and their beliefs are perverse and corrupt for, according to such extremists, these people are ignorant of political, social and economic regulations laid down by God which are not confined only to *Ibadat*. Allama Huzaibi comments on this view, "Everyone knows that authorities and legislatures have a right to frame laws and regulations on the principles and in the light of sanction by the Book and the *Sunnat* which lead to and subserve organisation of various aspects of political, economic and social life. There is not a trace of infidelity or polytheism in this belief. On the contrary, it is totally correct."[3]

Is the Relationship between man and God only of a servant and his Lord

We will discuss this theory later that to submit to the authority of any one other than God is as great a polytheism as to

1. Allama Huzaibi, *Duwatun La Quzat*, pp., 73-74
2. *Ibid.*, p. 74
3. *Ibid.*, p. 79

supplicate him for anything but, at first, we would draw the attention of the readers to the inference drawn from the passages quoted from the book—*Four Basic Quranic terms*—infact, from the whole of the book and numerous other writings of the learned author, that the only relation between God and man, is that of Lord and servant, a sovereign and His subject and amongst hundreds of names and attributes of God, the real attributes are of sovereignty and authority to be obeyed. In other words, the purpose of raising prophets, sending revelations, preaching and invitation is to stress the supremacy and authority of God and to lead life in accordance with this concept. It is true that belief in God and acceptance does entail belief in Lordship of God and servitude of man, but it is only a fraction and not the totality of the attributes and essence of God, of His relationship with His creatures and that of His creatures with Him. In reality the relationship between the Creator and the created, between the worshipped and the worshipper is far greater, wider, and deeper and far subtler and delicate than that of Lord and servant, a king and his subject, a commander and the commanded. The Quran has mentioned the names and attributes of God in such details and in such a fascinating and exquisite manner that certainly it cannot be its purpose to demand only this much from man that he should accept God as Supreme Authority and Supreme Ruler and not to associate any one else in this authority and rulership. For instance, I would cite the following verses of chapter 'The Exile'—

"He is Allah beside whom there is no other God—the knower of the visible and the invisible. He indeed is Compassionate, Merciful!

"He is Allah beside whom there is no God. He is the King, the Holy, the Perfect, the Granter of security, the Guardian, the Mighty, the Supreme, the Most High. Too Exalted is God in parity above all those they associate with

Him—He is Allah, the Creator, the Originator, the Fashioner! His are the names Excellent! Whatever is in the heavens and the earth extols Him! And He is the Mighty, the Wise."(Q. 59 : 22-24)

The demand of the Names and Attributes of God

Mention of these names and attributes of God and His way, with which the Holy Quran is replete, clearly demands that one should love Him with all his heart and soul, leave no endeavour in seeking Him and His pleasure, extol His names at every moment, hymn His praises in rapturous delight and have a living and constant consciousness of Him. Man is to fear Him, to beg and supplicate Him no doubt but he has also to fix his gaze on the wonder and beauty of His manifestations, to sacrifice every thing in His way and to be constantly prepared to make even the ultimate sacrifice. Those who limit the purpose and demand of the attributes and rights of God to sovereignty and supreme authority only may, I am afraid, be guilty of the foreboding of the Quran, 'No proper estimate do they form of God' (Q. 6 : 92).

In contrast to the ancient philosophical approach, which dwelt at length on negation of attributes and with brevity on recognition of His essence, the Quran has dwelt at length over the existence, and attributes of God. According to Shaikhul Islam Ibn Taimiya it is brief in negation and elaborate in positive assertion. The negation is summed up by saying, "There is nothing like Him" but in positing it, it adopts the style of the above cited verses of Chapter Exile. This is for the reason that attachment and devotion, love and fascination cannot develop without knowledge and recognition of attributes. The lives of the prophets, particularly of the last Prophet (Peace be on them), their deeds and preachings, their fervour of their prayers, their humility and contrition, their beseeching and supplications, their absorption in remembrance, the ardour of their love, their delight and comfort in recitation of His names, are reflections of the grandeur of the Attributes which can be again seen in the lives of the companions and the saints of the community. This was attained by their recognition of God not only as Supreme Authority and Ruler but also as the real Beloved and the beginning and end of all Beauty, Grandeur, Perfection and Benevolence.

Definition of Abudiyat and Ilah

Shaikhul-Islam Ibn Taimiyya, who was not a Sufi saint but, according to some, a dry Muhaddith and Alim, did not consider obedience, entreaty and humility enough for *abudiyat* (servitude) but considers it necessary that they should be accompanied by love and adoration of the worshipped. In his famours treatise '*Al-'Abudiyah*[1] he writes, "In the worship enjoined by the *shariat* there are elements of both obedience and love. Thus '*Ibadat* signifies both utmost obedience and utmost love." He proceeds to write, "If any one accepts subordination of a person but bears malice towards him he cannot be taken as a worshipper of that person and, likewise, if he loves something but does not recognise its greatness, he cannot be treated as a worshipper like one's love of his children or friends. Thus, in the servitude of God none of the two things is sufficient by itself. On the contrary, it is essential that man should regard God as the dearest and highest object of love as also the Greatest and the Most Magnificient Being."[4]

Not only this but in explaining '*Ilah*', he writes, "*Ilah* is that towards whom the heart turns in utmost love, greatest veneration, respect and esteem and in hope and fear and similar feelings."[2]

In another passage he clarifies that the relation between the worshipper and the worshipped is not merely that of a subject

1. *Al-'Abudiyah*, p. 6-7
2. *Ibid*, p. 12.

and a ruler, but is infinitely wider, deeper and comprehensive and in this association gnosis, penitence, love, sincerity and constant remembrance are all included. For a ruler humility, meekness, obedience and subordination alone are needed on the part of the subject. He writes, "God created His creatures for His servitude which covers gnosis, penitence, sincerety and love towards Him. In God's remembrance, hearts find consolation and in the Hereafter, the sight of His countenance would be the cool of their eyes. There will be nothing dearer to His servants than the sight of the Lord nor has He given in this world anything more valuable to man than faith in Him."[1] He states, "Without this type of servitude one can gain neither tranquillity nor success nor can he know what is real pleasure and bounty for he, who avoids servitude of God, has to face rigours of this life and sightlessness on the Day of Judgment."[2]

This definition of *Ilah* is althogether different from the one limited to sovereignty. The formal sovereign can invoke only complete subordination and loyalty but he cannot inspire love and devotion.

★★★

1. *Majmua Fatawah Shaikh ul-Islam Ahmad Ibn Taimiyah*, Vol. I, p. 23.
2. *Ibid*, p. 23.

CHAPTER V

The Real Function of Prophethood

IN trying to prove that sovereignty and the authority are indivisible, Maulana Maududi writes, "If anyone regards the word of someone else to be deserving of obedience without any sanction from God, he is as much guilty of the offence of *shirk* as the one who prays to or worships someone other than God. And if someone regards himself as the lord and master and absolute monarch of any part of the earth in the political sense, this act too amounts as much to a claim to godhood as it would if he were to tell people that he was their helper and patron and gurdian in the supernatural sense."[1]

This passage lends to the interpretation that polytheism (*shirk*) in the matter of orders and polytheism in divinity or worship stand on the same footing. In fact, the central theme of Maulana Maududi's writings is the politicai subjugation, acceptance of any one as supreme authority and to allow him the right

1. S. Abdul Ala Maududi, *Fou Basic Quranic Terms*, (Delhi, 1980), p. 28.

of legislation and compliance of his orders and he has wielded all the power of his facile pen on the subject. Any one confining himself to the study of writings of Mulana Maududi, and influnced intellectually by them would naturally attach greater importance to polytheism in the matter of orders and assign it the first place. If there are not other factors to work upon him or he has not the proper education and training, he would consider polytheism in worship or consideration of anyone, in a supernatural sense, as capable of giving help or entitled to be beseeched, supplicated or to be venerated and prostrated before as lesser evils, as a custom of the ancient days when intellect of man was still in its infancy and when culture and civilisation were at the elementary level and now that the world has progressed, to give attention to them, to contradict and confront them, is wasting time and energy and to be involved in a matter of lesser importance at the cost of the more important. In contrast, we see that inculcation of proper belief in respect of God, the relationship between the worshipped and the worshipper, servitude to God alone has been the foremost call of all the prophets and of their successors and heirs in all ages and climes and the main purpose of their lives. They always preached that God alone has the power to benefit or to injure and He alone deserves to be worshipped and supplicated and to be the centre of all attention. They forcefully countered the idolatry of their times expressing itself in the worship of idols, and of pious and venerated persons dead or alive. In the days of ignorance people had believed that God had conferred on these personages esteem and honour and the right to be adored and had given to them authority in particular matters and the stature to intercede on behalf of men much in the same way as a king confers authority on his governors and lays on them total responsibility in their areas barring in some very important matters.

If any one has studied the Quran, which is the completion of earlier scriptures, he will know for certain that its basic purpose is confrontation with idolatry, its abolition and to rescue people from its clutches. That was the main objective of the prophets, the reason for raising them, the foundation of their preachings, the end and the main purpose of their efforts. That was the central theme of their preachings, the axis round which revolved all their activities, the base from which they proceeded forward and to which they always returned, the beginning and the end of their endeavour. The Quran refers to it succinctly :

> "And no apostle have We sent before thee (O ! Prophet) to whom We did not reveal 'Verily, there is no god beside Me ; so be devoted to Me." (Q. 21 : 25).

At times it names a particular prophet and tells how he started his preachings from the concept of unity of God.[1]

The Quran treats this idolatry as the greatest polytheism and a falsehood and expounds its evil with great scorn and contempt. Thus the chapter *Victory* says :

> "This done, let him respect the sacred ordinances of God, since it will be pleasing to his Lord. Allowed to you are cattle (for food) except such parts of them as We specially mentioned to you (like their hair, skin and blood). This is how you should avoid filthy rites with idols and thus avoid also false invocations remaining firm in faith towards Him. And whoever associates aught with God, it is as if he has fallen from on high, and the birds have snatched him away or the wind has blown him to a distant place."
>
> (Q. 22:30,31)

1. For example : (Q. 11 : 25, 26, 50, 61, 84 ; Q. 26 : 69, 82 ; Q. 21 : 51, 54 ; Q. 19 : 41, 42 ; Q. 29 : 16, 17, 25 ; Q. 12 : 37–40)

The pattern and the spirit of Prophethood

This is the spirit of prophethood and the religion it ushers. In the sight of a prophet the most detestable and intolerable thing is idolatry of false deities, of self-created idols before which people prostrate themselves ; offer sacrifices and indulge in supplication and beseeching which is the exclusive prerogative of God. When the Holy Prophet (peace be on him) made his triumphant entry into Mecca with all authority and power, the first thing he did was to strike with his bow each of the three hundred and sixty idols installed in the Ka'aba reciting the verse, "And say, Truth is come and falsehood vanished. Verily falsehood is a thing which must vanish" (Q.17 : 81) and say, "The Word of truth has been delivered, and the (demon of) falsehood shall not put in its appearance now or hereafter" (Q. 34 : 49). All the idols tumbled down on their faces.[1] After the fall of Mecca he despatched parties in all directions for demolition of all idols, in particular, 'Lat', 'Uzza', and 'Manat' which were the favourites of the pagan Arabs. A spokesman announced in Mecca "Whosoever believes in God and the Hereafter, let him not allow existence of any idol in his house." He sent some companions to various tribes to demolish all the idols.[2] Hazrat Jarir bin Abdullah says, "In pagan days there was a temple called '*Zulkhalsa*', '*Ka'ba Yamaniya*' and '*Ka'ba Shamia*'. The Prophet said to me, 'Will you not comfort me by demolishing this temple," I took hundred horsemen of Ahmas with me, destroyed the temple, broke the idol into pieces and killed all the priests. On return I conveyed the good tiding to the Prophet who was very pleased over it and prayed for us and the people of Ahmas."[3] This is such a foremost task of prophethood that when the tribe of Thaqif requested the Prophet, after acceptance of Islam, to let their national idol 'Lat' remain for three years, he flatly refused

1. For details See *Zad-ul-Ma'ad*, vol. I, p. 424.
2. *Ibid*, p. 426.
3. *Sahih Bukhari*.

it. They came down to letting it stand for one month more but that was also refused. He immediately sent Abu Sufiyan and Mughira to destroy it straightaway. Abhorence and contempt for polytheism and worship of other than God was so strong that at the time of departure from this world his last worlds were, "May God destroy Christians and Jews who have made sepulchres of their prophets as places of worship."[1] Repeating this Hazrat Ayesha says, "The intention was that this community should not follow them and indulge in polytheism."[2] It shows that the Prophet regarded polytheism and its ways as an old and perennial failing and disease of nations and races and apprehended that it may lurk in some form. He, therefore, cautioned his followers against it even in his last breath. This is a message for the community, a responsibility and a trust. It also indicates that it is likely to subsist inspite of the advancement of the world and the progress of Islam. It is incumbent upon the Ulama and the vicegerents of the prophet to be always cautious and not to show any tolerance or relaxation in this regard.

Subsistence of Lat and Manat

This idolatry and polytheism are tokens of eternal and universal paganism which has not only been living in every age but has a youthful vigour. It is an ancient ailment and weakness of mankind which follows man in all walks of life, vicissitudes and revolutions of life. It incites God's wrath and indignation, it serves as the stumbling block in man's spiritual, moral and cultural progress and makes him fall from a high station to a botomless pit. Says the Quran, "Certainly We have created man in the goodliest form ; Then We let him go down to the lowest depth." (Q. 95 : 4,5) This paganism brings down man from the high station, where he was prostrated before by angels, to prostration before feeble creatures and base and insignificant objects.

1. *Muwatta Imam Malik.*
2. *Sahih Bukari.*

It stifles man's vitality, kills his capabilities, and ends man's belief in the Almighty, in self-confidence and self-realisation. It takes him away from the strong fortress of an Ever-seeing and Ever-hearing God, the Possessor of all knowledge and power, the Acme of benevolence and munificence, the loving and forgiving Lord. It deprives him of the benefit of His inexhaustible treasures and unbounded munificence and compels him to take refuge under the shelter of weak, helpless, destitute and abject creatures who have nothing to offer.
The Quran says :

> "He causeth the night to enter in upon the day, and causeth the day to enter in upon the night; and He hath engaged the sun and the moon to run their courses according to a prescribed schedule. Such indeed, is God, Your Lord; All power is His; But they on whom ye call beside God have no power over even the husk of a date stone; If ye cry to them, they cannot hear your cry, and even if they could ever hear, they cannot grant you what you ask for: and on the day of Resurrection, they will disown your setting them up as peers to God. And none can afford thee (O man) this information (in advance) except Him who is All informed. O Man, it is ye who truly are dependent on God for every thing while God is self-sufficient, the Praise-worthy." (Q. 35: 13, 14, 15)

The real target of Jehad of the Prophets.

It is this idolatry and polytheism in its defined and undefined form, which has been the target of assault by all the Prophets in all ages, environs and in all societies. It had roused the anger of the pagans and they had cried, "Would he replace all the gods by a single God: A strange thing indeed is this; And the leaders among them went away saying: 'Go and cling steadfastly to your gods. Indeed, the object of this design is clearly (against you). We never heard of this in any previous creed ; this is but an innovation." (Q. 38 : 5, 6, 7)

Any intelligent man who has studied the history of the Praphet's period and the companions will not have the slightest doubt that the companions were treating undue veneration and sanctification of dead or alive persons, prostration before them, making offerings before them, swearing by their names, worshipping them for achieving nearness to God, belief in their intercession, considering them as capable of conferring good or loss and requesting them for removal of their afflictions, as equivalent to worshipping of naked idols, stones and images. This is apparent from the trend of their sayings and there is no difference of opinion over it. This is the perpetual heritage of the Prophets, the basic theme of all reformative movements and religious exhortations till the end of the world. Says the Quran, "And this doctrine did he (Abraham) leave behind for his posterity that haply they might return to God." (Q. 43 : 25)

And this has been the way of all the reformers, crusaders and preachers.

★★★

CHAPTER VI

Distinction Between Open Polytheism and Political Submission

ALL other manifestations of paganism like servitude to other than God, acceptance of their power and laws contradictory to divine laws, submisson before such governments and acceptance of such laws and orders which do not conform to vicegerency of God, they are subordinate to idolatry and polytheism and come next to them. It would be tampering with religion if open polytheism is given lesser importance or is equated with political submission and rule or it is believed that polytheistic action and worship are a thing of the past or a relic of pagan days. This would be against facts and observation. This polytheism and worship of other than God is present even today in all its ancient forms. It can be seen in various forms at shrines of saints. There is harldy any waywardness, exaggeration, veneration and sanctity of other than God, bowing or prostration, sacrifice and offerings, beseeching and supplication, exhibition of hope and fear, all traditions of ancient paganism which cannot be noticed there. To consider them a thing of the past would be tantamount to have misgivings about the sacred efforts of the Prophets and their preachings and eternity of the Quran. It would be doubting that the ways of the Prophets were most excellent and pleasing to God and for which He gave so much aptitude, support, blessing, fruition and success more than which He did not accord to any other endeavour.

Worship in Maulana Maududi's view

According to Maulana Maududi the essence of *Rububiyat* is authority, and divinity and authority are inseparable and are synonymous in spirit and meaning[1] and that the Quran treats *Rububiyat* and sovereignty as synonymous[2] and thus the meaning and essence of *Ibadat* is obedience, and loyalty[3]. He was so much obssessed by this central point of divinity and providence, its speciality and single meaning and purpose that these acts, manifesations and ways of worship which are prescribed in the *Shariat* and required by the religion and were dear to the Prophet (peace be on him) lost their importance in his view. There are scores of verses and hundreds of *Ahadith* stressing their importance, narrating their excellence and exhorting us to vie in their adoption. Those who do not adopt them have been censured. But Maulana Maududi gives them secondary place and treats involvement in them as ignorance of the essence of religion and relic of the days of decadence. He has laid so much emphasis in explaining this central theme and its superiority (whose importance in its own place is not denied) that a vein of sarcasm and satire is discernible in his description of abundance of prayers and remembrance and other prescribed acts of worship, which is not his usual style. In dilating upon the three

1. For details see *Ar-Rad alal Bakri, Ar-Rad alal Ikhnai* of Ibn Taimiya and *Taqwiyut-ul- Islam* and *Sirat-e-Mustaqim* of Shah Ismail Shaheed.
2. Abul Ala Maududi: *Four Basic Quranic Terms*, pp. 28-29
3. *Ibid*: p. 76.

components of worship, he says "keep this meaning of *'Ibadat'* in mind and then give answers to my questions."

"What will you say about that servant who instead of performing the duties prescribed by his master stands all the time before him with folded hands and goes on chanting his name? The master orders him to go and redeem what is due to such and such persons but he sticks to his post, and bowing to the master salutes him ten times and again stands up with folded hands. The master instructs him to go and remove such and such wrongs but he does not budge an inch and starts prostrating before him. The master commands: "Cut off the hand of the thief". On hearing this order the servant still remains standing there, recites scores of time in an extremely melodious tone: "Cut off the hand of the thief," "Cut off the hand of the thief," but not once does he try to establish that system of government under which the hand of a thief can be severed. Can you say that this man is really serving his master? If any servant of yours were to adopt such an attitude, I do not know what will you say about it. But I am surprised at you that a servant of God who behaves like this is regarded by you as a devout worshipper of God! This heartless person reads from dawn to dusk, God knows how many times, the Divine injuctions in the Quran but never stirs himself to carry out those injunctions. On the other hand, he starts offering *Nawafil* after *Nawafil*, chants the name of God on a thousand-bead rosary and recites the Quran in a melodious tone. When you see him in this position you exclaim: "What a devout and pious person he is! "This misunderstanding arises because you do not know the correct meaning of *Ibadat*."[1]

Any one who knows even a little about the efforts for reform and religious invitation and who has read the writings or heard

1. S. Abdul Ala Maududi, *Fundamentals of Islam*, (Delhi 1979), pp 95-96

the speeches of profound Ulama, knows that they have invited people to act upon all the commandments of the *Shariat*, along with inculcation of the real spirit of prayers and fasting, to fashion their lives accordingly and to promulgate them among all men. They have treated such lives in which there is no conformity between the internal and external, between the body and the soul and which exhibits contrast between the verbal and the actual, between the exterior and the interior, as nothing short of hypocrisy. From the time of Hasan Basri till today they have been cautioning the Muslims against it and have been inviting them—'O ye who believe ! enter into the religion with fulness' (Q. 2 : 208) but they never adopted a style of expression displaying belittling or ridicule of engagement in worship and remembrance of God, His praise and glorification, or recitation of the Quran particularly in a period in which, due to various influences, devotional worship and remembrance are getting less and less and are receiving lesser importance. Materialistic and political ways of thinking have assumed the upper hand. A dozing person needs the excuse of a little push to go to sleep.

The Quran's Exhortation and Praise for Abundance of acts of Worship

In contrast, we find the Quran uses persuasion and appeal for profusion of such acts and has high praise for those performing it—

> "Who keeping themselves away from their beds, call on their Lord in awe and supplication and give to others in need of what We have provided them with." (Q. 32 : 16).

> "It is they who spend the night in prayer to their Lord, bowing down and standing." (Q. 25 . 64).

> "Those who pray for forgiveness at early dawn." (Q. 3 : 17).

"And the men who oft remember God and the women who oft remember—for all these, God holds out forgiveness and a great recompense." (Q. 33 : 35)

At places it orders—

"And extol Him profusely morning and evening."
(Q. 33 ; 42)

Seeking forgiveness of God, His remembrance and involvement in prayers are so pleasing to God that the Prophet of Islam (peace be on him), the most exalted of men and through whose instructions we have received this blessing, stressed them times out of number. At another place the Quran says, "And stand fast by those who call upon their Lord at morn and eve, seeking His approbation ; and let not thine eyes be turned away from them, with a view to gaining the adornments of the life of this world, and yield not to the bidding of him whose heart We have made neglectful of the remembrance of Us, and who followeth his own lusts and whose ways are unbridled." (Q. 18 ; 28)

Again it says, "And do not keep away from you those who cry to their Lord in the morning and in the evening, seeking His grace. Thou are not accountable for anything that they might have done, even as they are not accountable for anything that you may have done. Were thou to keep them away from thee, then thou indeed will be of the unjust." (Q 6 : 52)

The established *Ahadith* in respect of profusion of supererogatory prayers *(Nafil)*, remembrance of God and recitation of the Quran are so numerous that it is difficult to mention them. They can be seen in any book of Traditions. It would be sufficient to recount this *Hadith* only—

"Abdullah bin Busre reports that a person said to the Prophet (peace be on him), "O Apostle of God, I have known many commandments of Islam (but it is difficult for me to act on them simultaneously) therefore, tell me one thing which I can make the passion of my life." The Prophet said, "Keep your tongue wet with remembrance of God."[1]

Psychological effect of thc concept of God only as a Sovereign and Ultimate Authority

The effect of such type of thinking and writing, of which some examples have been presented above, would be (and their signs and indications have already started appearing) that the attachment of people, whose understanding of Islam would be limited to this kind of interpretation, with God would be limited, dry, soulless and of a formal character bereft of inner emotions demanded of a believer. If the purpose of apostleship is limited only to bringing about changes in this life, establishing culture on a sound basis and promoting reformative revolution and the whole thing is so stated that it heavily overlies the concept of love and approbation of God and expectations of final salvation, this would be the natural result. The whole train of thinking and effort, of struggle and action would get derailed from the rails of of faith in the unseen, desire for the Hereafter, and longing for love and pleasure of God so assiduously advocated by the Prophet and would start running on the tracks of desire for prestige, supremacy and authority and of materialism.

You may ponder over the following extracts and think for yourself what type of mentality would be developed by such an approach—

1. The real purpose of Islam is to produce a group which will establish human culture on the foundation of goodness and betterment.[2]

1. *Tirmidhi.*
2. *Islami Ibadat par ek Tahqiqi Nazar,* Vol. I, p. 75.

2. Prophets were sent one after another to establish such a social system in the world.[1]

3. The ultimate aim of all the prophets' mission in the world has been to establish the Kingdom of God on earth and enforce the system of life received from Him.[2]

Maulana Maududi writes, "With this object before them did all the Prophets endeavour to bring about political revolutions in their respective ages. Some of them were only able to prepare the ground, as Prophet Abraham; others succeeded in practically starting the revolutionary movement but their mission was terminated before they could establish the rule of God, as Prophet Jesus. But there were others who led their movement to its natural goal, culminating in the establishment of the Kingdom of God on the earth. In this latter category are included Prophet Joseph, Prophet Moses and our Holy Prophet Mohammad (peace be upon them all)."[3]

Are Islamic Ibadat and the four Pillars only Means and Methods

Add to this that this basic concept so obssesses the distinguished writer and exponent that to him appear all Islamic *Ibadat*, including the four pillars of Islam (Prayer, Fasting, Zakat and Haj), as only means and methods to attain the purpose, a sort of ground for practical traiuing and he expounds this view vehemently and repeatedly. At one place he writes, "This is why *Namaz*, Fasting, *Zakat* and *Haj* have been made compulsory *Ibadat*, but to call them *Ibadat* does not mean that they alone are *Ibadat*. On the contrary, it means that they prepare man for the real

1. *A Short History of the Revivalist Movement*, Maktaba Jamat-e-Islami, Pathankot, p. 21.
2. *Ibid*, p. 24
3. *Ibid*, pp. 24-25.

Ibadat (servitude) and they serve as an unavoidable traini · course."[1]

Maulana Maududi's statement clearly goes to suggest that the real objective is orderliness and subordination and establishment of the Kingdom of God and all the acts of worship including the prescribed acts are no more than means and methods therefor. But the Quran considers Jihad and the government only as the means and prop for establishment of prayers (*Salat*). Read the following verses of the chapter *Haj* and see for yourself what the Quran declares as the objective and what it treats as the means—

> "Permission is given (to fight) those who have taken up arms against you wrongfully. And verily, God is well able to give you succour, to those who have been driven forth from their homes for no reason other than this that they say, 'Our Lord is God'. Had not God repelled some men by others, cloisters and churches and synagogues and mosques, wherein the name of God is ever mentioned, would assuredly have been pulled down. Verily, him who helpeth God will God surely help : for, God is indeed Right, Powerfully Mighty. These are they, who, if We establish them in the land, will observe prayers and pay the poor-due, and enjoin what is right and forbid what is wrong. The final issue of all things rests with God." (Q. 22 : 39, 40, 41)

The example of the Prophet and his approach

Means have naturally a relationship with necessity and procedure and they can be considered as a passing phase. But they do not, by themselves, inspire a man to reach the pinnacle, to obtain pleasure and comfort from them or to improve them

1. *Islamic Ibadat per ek Tahqiqi Nazar*, Vol. I, p. 13, second Edition, Hyderabad,

for their own sake. If one does not look beyond the means, he cannot appreciate such *Ahadith* in which the state of prayers of the Prophet (peace be on him) has been described—"From his chest used to come a sound like a pot at the boil"[1] or his own saying, "The cool of my eyes lies in prayers"[2] or his asking Bilal, "Call for the prayers for my comfort."[3] Whenever he was placed in any predicament he would stand up for prayers.[4]

Even a glance at the Quran will confirm that attachment with God, devotion and service, and the four prescribed acts of worship are so required of man and consitute such a purpose of life that they alone will be questioned on the day of Resurrection and their neglect or abandonment will invite severe chastisement. The Quran says, "the dwellers of paradise will ask the inmates of hell, 'What has brought ye into Hell-fire?' They will reply, 'We were not of those who observed the prescribed prayers, and we were not of those who fed the poor, and we indulged in vain talk with idle thinkers, and we questioned the happening of the Day of Judgment, till death overtook us." (Q. 74 : 42–47)

About the infidel it says, "This is he who had neither believed in the truth nor observed the prayers *(Namaz)* but had called the Truth a lie and turned his back and had gone back to his people with haughty bearing." (Q. 75 : 31–33)

This should convince any one that acts of worships, and the pillars of religion have the fundamental and pivotal position in the whole structure of the religion. They will be questioned and they will have to be accounted for it. The rest of the things

1. *Abu Dand : Trimidhi*
2. *Nissai*
3. *Abu Daud*
4. *Ibid.*

like establishment of the kindgom of God and evolution of human culture, on the basis of goodness and betterment, are no more than means and occupy secondary position.

Psychological effect of treating Ibadat and Arkan only as means.

Means provide occupation to the point of necessity but they do not provide devotion and a heavy involvement. If *Ibadat* and *Arkan* were only means then the length of the *Salat* of the Prophet (peace be on him) and his standing erect therein for such long periods that his feet used to get swollen,[1] his inducement and persuasion for abundance of supererogatory prayers yielding special attachment,[2] his eager waiting for the next prescribed prayers after the performance of one,[3] would not have been so intense and keen. On the day of reckoning among those fortunate persons who would be under the Divine shade would be the man whose heart remained attached to the mosque.[4] The Prophet (peace be on him) had directed his followers to perform prostrations in abundance saying that when you perform one prostration, God elevates you one degree and forgives one sin.[5]

On top of it, the Quran's description of devout believers (*Mominin*) that 'they spend their nights in prostration and in standing posture,' and 'who keep themselves away from their beds during the night,' clearly indicates that the status of prayers is not merely orderliness and subordination and esta-bishment of the kingdom of God but they are an end by them-selves. If they are means of anything they are the means of attaining the pleasure of God and His nearness. To consider

1. *Sahih Bukhari* and *Muslim, Tirmidhi* and *Nassai* on the authority of Mughira bin Shuaba.
2. *Sahihain*
3. *Muslim.*
4. *Sahihain*
5. *Muslim, Ibn Maja. Nassai, Musnad* on the authority of Thauban and Abu Darda.

them only as means in the fashion of Maulana Maududi can never generate attachment of the heart in prayers, any spirit or state, any humility and submissiveness, meekness and penitence, contemplation and concentration, constant remembrance, sincerity, faith and self-assessment. This way would finish the deep realisation of its necessity and importance, longing and concern for progress and perfection, high resolve, the search of guides who have attained distinction in this field and who can assist and guide in that direction.

The sub-continent of India has been the biggest centre during the past centuries of elevated souls, who insisted upon and taught creation of quality and spirit in worship, of contrition and meekness and of sincerity and self-assessment in action. This produced many masters and experts for fashioning and perfection of inner state of man and advantage was taken of them by many far-flung parts of the Islamic world and even by those countries which had been themselves centres of learning. A big difficulty, however, arose that because of treatment of worship as mere means and by styling the art and practice of purification of *nafs* as *Tasawwuf* and by highlighting the weaknesses and blemishes of some votaries thereof, the more orthodox developed such a dread and ridicule for them that they were not prepared even to hear their names.[1] When Maulana Maududi himself starts writing about them he adopts a strain altogether different from his usual style. For instance, writing about the revivalist accomplishment of Mujuddid Alf Sani, Shah Waliullah and his successors who believed in and practised and taught *Tasawwuf* to others, he writes, "Just as a pure and lawful thing like water is prohibited when it is deemed to be harmful to a patient, similarly the cult

1. There is no art in the world and no vocation of life in which do not exist the real, the spurious, the perfect and the defective. the adept and the quack but that does not argue scoring out the whole class or overlooking of totality.

of *Tasawwuf*, though permissible, needs to be eschewed and laid aside. For through it Muslims have become addicted to a kind of intoxication which has lulled them to sleep and sapped them of life and reality for centuries."[1]

★★★

1. S. Abul Ala Maududi, *A Short Histroy of the Revivalist Movement in Islam*, (Lahore 1963) p. 106.

CHAPTER VII

Presumption of Stagnation, Indolence and escapism

THE fact is that Maulana Maududi has accepted, as a self-evident truth with no scope for any discussion or review, that *Tasawwuf* is yet another name for lethargy and inaction, escape from the realities of life, and not only withdrawl from the struggle between the truth and falsehood, but acceptance of defeat before the forces of falsehood and a collusion with them. According to him, they are necessary corollaries and inseparable from one another. He writes at one place, "Is there any proof in mystical literature that establishment of religion, in all its connotations, was ever before these illustrious people from whom the ways of *Sufism* have been derived? Is there any trace that for this purpose volunteers were prepared and did those volunteers and members do anything or were their methods ever found useful in this pursuit."[1]

1. Abul Ala Maududi: *Rasail wa Masail*, Vol.II, p. 602.

Two examples from the history of Jihad and endeavour

Instead of entering into the vast record of history and citing the names of crusaders, leaders and revolutionaries and protagonists of Islam who combined the virtues of martial bravery and ascetic devotee, of valiant warriors of battlefields and of whole-night worshippers of mosques, who threw gauntlets at every gibbet and halter, at every affliction and sorrow and were ever prepared, along with comrades trained by them, to confront forces of falsehood and evil, we are presenting in reply to this imputation the examples of two persons only, Saiyid Ahmad Shaheed and Maulana Ismail Shaheed from Maulana's own book '*Tajdid wa Ahya-e-Din (A Short History of Revivalist Movement in Islam)* about whom he has written that they gave the medicine to the patients which had proved fatal in the disease and that 'the custom of directorship and discipleship *(peri muredi)* was current in their movement.' However, acknowledging the extraordinary talents and efforts of Saiyid Sahib and their impact, Maulana Maududi writes.,—

1. They raised a strong movement for the reformation of the religious, moral and social affairs of the common people. Wherever their good influence reached lives were completely so revolutionised that they reminded once again of the lives of the Holy Prophet's Companions.

2. They made large-scale preparations for *Jihad* at a difficult time (beginning of the 19th century) when India was fast heading towards total collapse and disintegration; and they displayed marvellous organizational skill and ability in this work. That they selected the north-western India (now West Pakistan), for the launching of their campaign clearly shows their deep knowledge of war strategy in those days. Politically as well as geographically there could be no better starting point. Then, they tried to observe

throghout *Jihad* all the moral principles and war tactics which are the hallmark of a *Mujahid* that distiguishes him from a world seeking fighter. Thus they demostrated once again the real Islamic spirit before the world. They did not fight for the sake of wealth or territory, national pride or any other worldly greed; they fought in the way of Allah. *The only objective before them was to deliver the masses af the people from the yoke of un-Godly rule, and establish that system of government which accords with the will of the Creator and real Sovereign.* With this object in view they first invited the people, according to rule, to accept Islam or to pay *Jizyah*, and then took up arms as a last resort. And when they took up arms they scrupulously observed the civilized law of war taught by Islam; they did not commit any wild or savage act; and they did not enter a township to destroy and shed blood but to reform and make peace. Their army was neither accompanied by barrels of wine, nor attended by musical band and prostitutes to turn their camps into brothels. Not even a single instance has been reported that the *Mujahidin* passed through a locality and the inhabitants complained about the molestation of their women and the plunder of their properties. On the contrary, these soldiers of God spent their day time on horse-back and nights in prayers; they feared God and remembered the Day of Judgment always; and they were firm on the way of truth and justice in all circumstances, favourable or unfavourable. If they suffered a defeat they did not lose heart and show cowardice ; if they came out triumphant they did not feel proud and behave like tyrants. History bears evidence that the soil of the sub-continent had neither witnessed the real Islamic *Jihad* before them nor has ever seen such a phenomenon after them,

3. *When they got a chance to establish their rule in a limited territory they established it on the basis of "Caliphate*

after the pattern af Prophethood." It was characteristic of the same pious and God-fearing control, the same kind of equality and advisory body, and the same execution of justice and enforcement of *Shariah* punishments. Property was lawfully seized and justly disposed of, the oppressed were protected though they be weak, and the oppressors were crushed though they be strong. The rulers feared God and executed the Governmental business with perfect morality. Thus they demonstrated and revived once again the type of rule established and guided by Abu Bakr Siddiq and Umar Faruq (may God be pleased with them)."[1]

Was not the struggle of these martyrs for perpetuation of the religion

We can respectfully ask whether the efforts of Saiyid Sahib, his comrade and disciple Maulana Ismail Shaheed were not for perpetuation of religion, who endeavoured to reform morality and daily business, to revolutionise the lives of people, who prepared the people for Jihad and to employ it for rightful purpose, who tried to establish a system of gevernment in keeping with the ordinances of God and the pattern of the early Caliphate? Was this not accomplished by the persons who not only believed in and practiced *Tasawwuf* but also taught and preached it to others.?

Naturally and logically only those could perform this stupendous task who had freed themselves from the shackles of the *Nafs*, the attraction of the world and love of pelf and position, the desire of longevity or in Quranic language, "Every one (of the polytheists) wishes that he may live for a thousand years" and from the root of every hair of whom comes the cry: 'Tomorrow we shall meet our friends, i.e. the Prophet and his

1. S. Abu Ala Maududi, *A Short History of the Revivalist Movement in Islam,* (Lahore, 1963) pp. 101-103 *(Italics ours)*

comrades'.[1] At this place I would like to reproduce what I have written elsewhere, "The fact is by religious exercises, abstinence and hard struggle, by purification of the *Nafs,* and nearness of God, that love of God, ardour and longing are generated that every hair calls out—

"What have we that we may sacrifice except this borrowed life."

It is for this reason that the end result of all spiritual progress and inner perfection is the longing for martyrdom and the culmination of endeavour (*mujahida*) is *Jihad.*

"Considered pyschologically, certitude and love are the pedestal from which rises the falcon of *Jihad* and hard struggle. Only he can escape from the baseness of desires of the self, habits and customs, material gains and expediency, and personal interests in whom have been generated the mercurial agility of quicksilver and the restlessness of lightning.

"It is the profoundest experience of human life that mere knowledge, investigation and research, bare laws and regulations, order and system, are not sufficient for staking one's life or even for producing the spirit and willingness to sacrifice. It requires greater motivation, a stronger devotion, a spiritual ambition and certainty of nonmaterial gains in the face of which this life appears a cumbersome burden. It is for this state that a poet has said.

"In the realm of love,
the value of life lies
in the lane of the beloved.
Because of this glad tiding
the head seems to be a burden
on the shoulders."[2]

1. These words were uttered by Hazrat Bilal on his last breath and similar words were uttered by many a saint
2. Compilation of articles, *Tasawwuf kya Hai',* by Maulana Mohd. Manzoor Nomani.

If anyone attained anything, it was the enraptured mystic

As against this, let any one cite just one example of establishment and expansion of Islam done by any person or group who was unacquainted with *Tasawwuf* or who denied and opposed it. The whole history of Islam is before us, before Maulana Maududi and hundereds of scholars and talented persons. Can any one point out any religious movement or struggle which was not 'contaminated' by the 'germs' of *Tasawwuf* and was inspired and led by men through pure acumen, study and reflection and who had kept themselves aloof from the company of sipritual masters and training of the inner self.[1]

On the contrary, we find at least from the beginning of the nineteenth century till the middle of the twentieth century that those who confronted the imperialistic forces, prepared the ground for *Jihad*, inspired the spirit of intrepidity and emanicipation in the Muslim society, of selflessness and sacrifice, of high resolution, courage, venture and daring and of staking one's life and who frustrated and demoralised the biggest western powers, inspite of the fewness of their comrades and valiant soldiers and the paucity of resources and equipment, and for years and years saved their countries from being swallowed by western powers, they were all connected with some sufistic order (*Silsilah*), had received training from spiritual preceptors and directors and had treaded the path of '*Ihsan*' and gnosis.

For example, we can mention the names of the famous *Mujahid* Amir Abdul Qadir of Algeria, Muhammad Ahmad (Mahdi of Sudan) the greatest opponent and challenger of the

1. A few names can no doubt be mentioned of persons who did laudable but fragmentary work for correction of beliefs or expansiou of Islam but firstly there is no proof that their endeavour had the dimension of Jihad or revival of Islamic Caliphate and secondly, even if they were unacquainted with *Tasawwuf*, they had reached the state of attachment with God and close connection which is the goal of purification of the *nafs*.

British power in Sudan, the great Mujahid Ahmad Sharif Sanusi of Tripoli, the great valiant Shaikh Shamil Naqshbandi of Taghisian, the founder of Ikhwanul Muslimin (the greatest Islamic movement of recent times) Shaikh Hasan-al-Banna of Egypt, and in India, of Maulana Yahya Ali Azimabadi, the greatest victim of the wrath and persecution of the imperialist power, of Maulana Ahmadullah and Molvi Muhammad Jafar Thaneswari, the prisoners of Andaman, the standard bearers of the 1857 Revolution—Ahmadullah Shah of Madras, Maulana Liaqat Ali of Allahabad, the martyr Hafiz Zamin of Shamli, the leader and Mujahid Haji Imdadullah Muhajir Makki and his disciples Maulana Muhammad Qasim Nanatawi, Maulana Rashid Ahmad of Gangoh, the inspiring force behind the Khilafat movement and the greatest opponent of the British power Shaikhul Hind Maulana Mahmud Hasan of Deoband and his successor Maulana Saiyid Husain Ahmad Madani, Haji Sahib Tarangzai of the Frontier Province, and Maulana Saifur Rahman of Tonk.[1] Were these people victims of stagnation and indolence, examples of defeatism and escape from the field of struggle, of compromise with forces of falsehood, of renunciation from this 'debased world' and of flight to the 'Sanctum of Reality', and of spending their lives on prayer mats and carpets of spiritual predecessors ?

The detached verdict of history

History deals with a subject which is factual, realistic and sensitive. It does not admit any concession by way of tolerance and gives its critical assessment irrespective of the stature of thinkers, scholars or protagonists of religion.

The duty of presentation of Religion in the light of history & Shariat

There is no difference of opinion, in my knowledge, amongst the Ulama of Islam about the necessity of struggle for acquiring

1. For details see the author's book '*Tazkia aur Ihsan*', and his article '*Ahle Tasawwuf aur Dini Jadd-o-Jahad* in the book '*Tasawwuf Kya Hai*.

power and authority to enable enforcement of divine laws and authority in the society and to see that no parallel power, authority or system remains in opposition to create tensions, conflicts and discord towards which the Quran refers—

> "O Believers ! you have no alternative except to fight till persecution ceases and the true way of life is pursued in absolute devotion of God." (Q. 8 : 39)

It is also necessary to attain such power and position that not only propagation of Islam can be done but there should also be authority to enforce what is commanded and what is prohibited—

> "(O believers) Ye are the best of the communities raised up to be a model for mankind. Ye enjoin the right and forbid the wrong, and ye repose faith in God:" (Q. 3 : 110)

> "Let there be a band of people among you who shall call men to goodness and enjoin what is recognised on all hands to be good and forbid what is considered to be evil." (Q. 3 : 104)

Acquisition of this type of authority and power is the demand of the Quran and no negligence or lethargy in that regard is permissible. The consequences of abandoning this responsibility, appearing in the form of poverty of Islam, victimisation of Muslims, suspension of the ordinances of God resulting in disorderliness and chaos, withdrawl of God's help and deprivation of His blessings, have been spelt out in detail in the Quran and *Ahadith*. It is for this reason that so much emphasis has been laid on the establishment of caliphate that a life without it and a death outside the system have been described pagan way of life and death[1]. On that basis, the companions, after the death of the

1. For details see my article appearing as Introduction to *Tarikh Imarat-e-Shariya*.

Holy Prophet (peace be on him) gave foremost attention and priority to it, Hazrat Ali struggled hard and longed to bring it on the right lines, Hazrat Husain sacrificed his life and in every age the jurists and the resolute persons of the community staked everything for it and due to neglect of which the whole world of Islam is in disgrace and has lost prestige and influence.

But all this only constitutes an important and unending means and is certainly not the whole of religion or the foremost objective. The erudite Ulama of Islam who reflect on the Book and the *Sunnat,* whose knowledge of religion is based on deep and wide study of the Book and the *Sunnat*, of the life history of the Prophet and the accounts of the companions, whose scholarly trend and pattern of thinking and ways of invitation had developed in the school of prophetic tradition, un-influenced by any external education or discipline and which was not just a reaction against any current evil, wrong or misconceived movement, when such persons talk over the subject to stress its necessity and importance or lament over its disappearance and the apathy of the Muslims, their language, the style of their diction, their emotions and motivating factors are altogether different.[1]

The clear though subtle distinction between the goal and the means is maintained in their writings which clearly show that

1. What the author has written about the basic difference between the Prophets and other reformers in his book entitled *Islamic Concept of Prophethood* (Lucknow, 1976, p. 42) is reproduced below.

   "This basic but subtle difference is very often overlooked by those writers and scholars of the Muslim world who try to present an Islamic view of the life and social order with an eye to fight the cultural and politieal ascendancy of the West. Anyone who has made a deep study of the Quran and the *Sunnah* and is also aware of the forceful impact of modern thought and culture, but has had the moral and intellectual grit to steer clear of the contaminating influences of modernism, can easily detect the traces of Western ideology and thought in the writings of such Muslim reformers."

the purpose of struggle for gaining power and authority, of establishment of caliphate and Imarate is solely for gaining God's pleasure, for following the Prophets' ways (peace be on him), for supremacy of religion and establishment of its basic tenets, for revival of religious knowledge and for the sake of establishment of the right and abolition of the wrong. Hakim-ul-Islam Hazrat Shah Wali Ullah Dehlavi in his unrivalled book *Izalat-ul-Khifa* describes Caliphate as follows—

> 'Caliphate means supreme authority for establishment of religion in a way that it revives religious learning and establishes the tenets of Islam, for arranging *Jihad* and connected matters (i.e., organisation of forces, recruitment of volunteers and distribution of spoils of war, juridical code and penal laws are promulgated, tyranny is wiped off, establishment of right and abolition of wrong is practised all in the ways of the Prophet of Islam (peace be on him).'[1] Explaining it he says, "If all these purposes and sectors of caliphate are to be expressed in a few words which can cover the totality of these parts and are the genus of the ramifications they are 'Establishment of Religion".[2] Then he says, 'Establishing such an organisation and administration is incumbent upon the Muslims till the Doomsday as *'Wajib-bil-Kifayah.*'[3]

After giving legal arguments he writes, "*Jihad* and justice, revival of religious learning, tenets of Islam, protection of Islam and Muslims from domination by infidels is a duty cast upon Muslims by God and this cannot be done without the selection and appointment of an Imam. It is an established principle that the preliminaries of an obligation (*Wajib)* are also obligatory (i.e. if an obligation cannot be discharged without some preli-

1. Shah Waliullah, *Izalatul Khifa*, p. 2
2. Shah Waliullah, *Izalatul Khifa*, p. 2
3. *Ibid.*

minary steps, those steps are also obligatory."[1]

At this place it is necessary to explain that the words 'establishment of religion' are not synonymous with efforts for establishment of the kingdom of God. They have a much wider connotation. What is usually described in the literature of the *Jama'at* are branches of establishment of religion as mentioned by Shah Waliullah. The words, "*Iqamat-i-Din*' have been used in the Quran only at one place in the chapter Shura verse 13—

> "To you hath He prescribed the Faith which He had commanded unto Noah, and which, We have revealed to thee and which We had commanded unto Abraham and Moses and Jesus enjoining, 'Establish this Faith and do not divide yourselves into sects.' Disconcerting to the polytheists is that (the faith) to which thou callest them. God draweth to Himself whom He Wills and guideth to Himself whosoever turns to Him."

The context of this verse tells us that the whole of the religion and its teachings (belief, worship and daily business are meant and not only caliphate, government, or acquisition of power and authority. Allama Allusi in his famous commentary '*Ruh-ul-Ma'ani* in explaining 'establishment of religion' says, 'Here by *Din* is meant the religion of Islam which comprises belief in Unity of God, and His obedience, His books and apostles and the Hereafter and all the beliefs and actions by which a person becomes a devout believer. By establishment of religion is meant preservation of the purity of its tenets from accretions and distortions and steadfast adherence to it.'[1]

Later on, the illustrious grandson of Shah Waliullah,

1. Shah Waliullah, *Izalatul Khifa*, p. 2
1. *Ruh-ul-Ma'ani*, Vol. VII, p. 513.

Maulana Ismail Shaheed, wrote a full book on the subject by the name of *Mansab-i-Imamat*, which occupies a distinguished position in Islamic literature and has got few equals in the force of its expression, the logic and strength of its reasoning and in elucidation of subtle points.

In the first half of the thirteenth century Hijri, Hazrat Saiyid Ahmad Shaheed had given particular attention to this aspect of establishment of religion in India. For acquiring power and authority for Islam, for creation of the necessary climate and environment and for collection of the necessary material and resources, he made such organised, resolute and consistent efforts and extended invitation to others for it with such grandeur, zeal and fervour that its example is found neither in recent history nor in the years preceding. His famous biographer, Maulana Ghulam Rasul Mehr, has rightly written in *Saiyid Ahmad Shaheed.*

> "This is a chapter of the history of India-Pakistan of the era which is regarded as the period of decline of Muslims but will any truth-loving and truth discerning person have hesitation in acknowledging that any period of the rise of Muslims was not, in principle, more glorious than this period. Judgement is not based on results but on the character of efforts made, the steadfastness shown and the determination exhibited in the right cause. Can any one say that we can find similar instances of height of endeavour, height of valour and steadfastness in the accounts of days of ascendancy wherein the object was religion and religion alone."[1]

We are now reproducing some extracts of Sayid Sahib's letters to Muslim princes and the Ulamas and the nobility of the sub-continent. They will reveal the spirit, the real

1. Ghulam Rasul Mehr : *Sayid Ahmad Shaheed*, Lahore edition.

objective and the nature of thinking which was upholding the whole struggle. The real objective was obedience of God's commandments and the pleasure of God and what was inspiring it was the decadence and helplessness of the Muslims. Nothing else was in view besides the elevation of the Word of God, revival of *Sunnat* and rescue of the Islamic territory. He took the steps in the conviction that religion can flourish only in Muslim domain and the ordinances of *Sharia* cannot be enforced without authority and they are no more than servants of those commandments and seekers of God's pleasure. In a letter to the Ulama and the nobles of the Frontier Province he wrote, "This destitute has relied on God's promise,[1] has made obedience of His commands his sole ambition, having relegated everything besides God to the background and closed his eyes to the surroundings. Keeping the right way of the pleasure of God in view he is traversing the path in full confidence, hope and felicity."[2]

In the same letter he writes, "We are God's servants and members of the Prophet's *Ummat* and undoubtedly claim to be Muslims and count ourselves among the followers of the Prophet. When on the point of *Jehad* we have accepted the word of God as decisive and the Prophet (peace be on him) as true, we have inevitably girded our loins to fulfil the commandment of God and have come out to follow the way of the Prophet."[3]

In a letter to Shah Sulaiman, the ruler of Chitral, he categorically expresses his real inspiration and spirit and says that he is not seeking power and position and his object is only enforcement of God's commands and revival of *Sunnat*.

1. The promise of God's pleasure and assistance on such efforts made in the Quran and the *Ahadith*.
2. *Seerat Saiyid Ahmad Shaheed*, Vol. I, p. 386.
3. *Ibid*, p. 387

In regard to rule and justice he only wants observance of true *Shariat* and the holy *Sunnat*. He writes, "This destitute has nothing to do with riches and pelf, or acquistion of rulership and government. If any one amongst my brothers of the faith can liberate the country, give currency to the commands of God and propagate the *Sunnat* of the Holy Prophet (peace be on him) and in governmental rule and justice can be guided by *Sharia*, it would mean the success of my efforts and the fulfilment of my ambition."[1]

While emphasizing it, the fervour of his faith and the zeal of his sincerity reach their heights. While writing to Sardar Sultan Muhammad Khan and Sardar Saiyid Muhammad Khan, the rulers of Peshawar, he worte the stirring sentences, "The crown of Faridun and the throne of Alexander have not the value of a grain of barley in my view nor do I attach any significance to the kingdoms of Caeser and Khusros. My only desire is that with majority of the people, in fact in the whole world, God's commandment, called the *Sharia*, should get into vogue, without any opposition, either through my hands or through some one else's."[2]

From his letter it appears that the real motivation for his struggle and the deciding factor in this regard was his concept of religion that without authority and rule, a good part of Islamic *Sharia* and command of God cannot be implemented and remains in abeyance. The Muslims remain helpless and see with their own eyes the gradual extinction of Islamic ways, the desecration and demolition of their places of worship and can do nothing about it. Writing again to the above rulers he says, "Those commandments of religion, which pertain to rulership, become incapable of execution in the absence of dominion. The Muslims are thwarted in their affairs, and at

1. *Seerat Saiyid Ahmad Shaheed*, p. 391
2. *Ibid*, p. 392

the hands of the turbulent infidels humiliation of Muslims, adversity, dishonouring of the ways of the sacred *Shariat* and desecration and destruction of their mosques are perpetrated."[1]

★★★

1. *Ibid*, p. 391

CHAPTER VIII

Establishment of Religion with Sagacity of Religion

BUT this part of establishment of religion (efforts to attain dominance and authority) is not like inflexible iron structure which can break but cannot bend or expand. In regard to those on whose sincerity, erudition, and expertness in Islamic Jurisprudence we can safely depend, on the basis of positive evidence and appearances, those who had shown no laxity and had believed in rigid application, we will have to concede the right to them that they adopted the most suitable ways in the conditions of their times for attaining the objective. They did not spare any effort for result is always the objective and not the means, constructive activity and not destructive is the course and positive achievements and not negation are the target. No intelligent person can say that it was necessary for these hard workers to spend their total energy and time in demolition of the edifice, in which had appeared some weaknesses or which was being misused. They could not be even sure whether they would get opportunity to build it anew. In the presence of vast and strong Muslim states, whose heads had certain abilities and facilities, if they, instead of presenting total opposition, took up the course of counselling and rectification, reformation instead of elimination, we cannot say that they had forgotten their duty of establishment of religion and were guilty of 'collaboration in commission of sins and tyranny.' They endeavoured to reform the society, to turn it from pagan to Islamic ways, to the worship of God rather than worship of the self, and bent all their energies physical, spiritual, literary and oratory in this task for the right Islamic sociely is the base and the level ground which can support heavy and lofty buildings and can accept and bear any sound leadership. Side by side they maintained liaison with the central leadership and the seat of the government, drew up exhaustive codes for the government to rule and decide in accordance with the *Shariat* to control administraiton and order and to collect revenues. By establishing their seflessness and sincerity, their moral and spiritual stature on the rulers of the day, they repeatedly saved them from taking measures likely to injure Islam and the Muslims. They got the *Sharia* and penal laws promulgated through these rulers, prepared them for combating forces inimical to Islam, and were responsible for *Jihad* and expansion of the Islamic Empire. They supplied to the rulers God-fearing, trust worthy and capable volunteers whom they had disciplined for years. At times it also happened through their efforts that the reins of government were transferred from irreligious rulers to pious successors, from opponents of Islam to protectors of Islam, from destroyers of religion to champions of religion. We will have to treat all of them as standard-bearers of the struggle for establishment of religion, as loyal soldiers of the auspicious regiment of revivalists and renovators and we cannot possibly regard the neglectful of their duty and exclude them from the auspicious list on the ground that they failed to establish an ideal kingdom of God.

Even Maulana Maududi himself forcefully acknowledges the necessity of practical skill, of appreciation and understanding of the circumstances and of devising policies and shaping action in accordance therewith and calls it practical strategy. At one place he writes, "Tactics and practical strategy determine what steps should be taken in advance to reach the goal, what opportunities should be availed of, what rules of conduct should be flexible and where flexibility should be introduced for the sake of the higher objective."[1]

At another place he writes, "Briefly, practical strategy means that in establishing religion and promulgating the *Sharia* laws we should keep in view the circumstances in which we are living and juristic verdicts and course of action should be so altered and modelled that the objects of *Sharia* are properly fulfilled and not that they should be sacrified by application of rules and orders in un-favourable circumstances."[2]

At yet another place he writes, "whoever has to take practical steps for establishing religion, whether an individual, party or state, he has necessarily to work with sagacity in the prevailing circumstances and not only to make suitable changes in lawful plans, on the demand of the occasion, but also to uitlise relaxations permitted by the *Sharia* which even the prophets and the companions had not hesitated to utilise."[3]

If this principle is accepted, and we have confidence in the sincerity, expertness in Islamic jurisprudence and the character of their endeavour as testified by their whole lives, then in the light of authentic history, we will have to treat as dedicated marchers of the way all the *mujtahidin* who deduced answers to issues from

1. Maulana Maududi : *Tafhimat*, Vol. III pp. 91, 92, Delhi Edition.
2. *Ibid*, : p. 183 ;
3. *Ibid*, : p. 189.

the Quran and *Sunnat* and guided the community, the traditionists who collected, analysed and compiled the *Ahadith*, the jurists who compiled laws of taxation. In the same group stand the elevated souls who stopped the Muslims from being swept in the current of materialism, abundance of wealth, frequency and dimensions of conquests or rescued them from selfishness and hankering after power or bowing before power and authority or running after posts and positions and sacrificing their faith, principles and conscience in the process. This august group also includes those stalwarts who from declining and deteriorating society raised people of character and stamina and placed them at dangerous frontiers and decisive fronts, who converted, through their quiet endeavour, whole of non-Muslim communities, often inimical to Islam, the victors of Muslims, royal families and influential people to Islam, those who won the hearts of kings, rulers and the common people by their moral and spiritual stature, selflessness and sincerity and persuaded them to observe justice and equity, to promulgate ordinances of the *Shariat*, to abolish evils and innovations, and those who preferred collective good to intense personal involvement in worship and with God and repeatedly placed themeselves in danger, as also those who shaped the thinking of men, arranged for their training and discipline on the basis of learning and knowledge for bringing about a righteous revolution and establishing Muslim rule on sound foundation. They might have belonged to any group or might have been called by any title, they were the real men who discharged the obligation of establishing religion in their times and circumstances, The difference is only this that history throws bright light on the accounts of some, while those of others are not complied in the well-known books of history and we have to refer to letters, annals and unpublished books. When we study them we find that in every age there was endeavour within the limitations of resources and the righteous Ulama played their part and gained God's pleasure and satisfaction and several steadfast amongst them carried the work to its goal which is still a far cry for many parties and groups working in the sub-continent and Islamic countries with or without any labels, and no body knows if they will be able to reach the destination.

So far as Hazrat Saiyid Ahmad Shaheed and his companions are concerned, they employed all their energies and capabilities to the fulfilment of this task and spared no means and efforts which could be profitable in gaining the objective and ultimately made the supreme sacrifice.

★★★

CHAPTER IX

The last request

THE submissions, which have the character of some analytical expositions in explaining and interpreting religious truths and purposes, may be unpleasnt to those who are not used to making distinction between difference in principle and personal opposition and who construe any difference in opinion, with any investigation or point of view held by any servant of the religion or by the leader of any movement which is yielding any type of religious, communal or political benefit, as injury to the cause of Islam and hindrance to collectivisation. It cannot be denied that, at times, the difference of opinion and refutation have been utilised for political gains but the fact remains that differences in points of view and enquiry and their expression, purely in the interest of the religion and the Muslims, have not only been the practice at all times but have helped greatly prevention of partial distortions in the religion and total deflection by the community.

What to say of the leading *Mujtahidin* about whom no suspicion of any blemish or of selfishness, jealousy and contemporaneity can possibly be raised, even those who are counted after them in stature, knowledge and popularity, not only tolerated the differences of opinion and results of enquiry but welcomed them and thanked their critics. Their followers also accepted the criticism and investigations of their contemporaries of the same profession with largeness of heart and gave serious thought to them and did not impute any personal motive or lay the charge of injuring Islamic interest. The criticism of Ibn Jauzi and Imam Ibn Taimiyya, of Hujjat-ul-Islam Imam Ghazali and the criticism of Shaikh-ul-Islam Ibn Taimiyya by his contemporaries, who acknowledged his vast erudition, rare acumen and undoubted sincerity, (like Allama Zahbi, Ibn Daqiq-ul-eid and others) are instances in point. In the same way, the great Sufis differed from one another but with full deference and veneration and refuted some findings and 'states' discovered by others. If sincerity, true quest, preservation from any shadow of distortion, ascendancy of Islam are kept in view and it is fully believed that only a prophet is innocent, then not only such criticism and analysis will not be taken amiss but should be gratifying that they would help in understanding of the religion and preservation and protection of Islam. This serves to prove that the objective is adherence to truth, and pleasure of God and not of glorification of personalities or adherence to letter and bigotry.

The history of schism in Islam reveals that the foundations of many groups and sects rested on honesty of purpose, spirit of reform and inclination to remove weaknesses, stagnation and exaggeration. The founders thereof had exhorted the people to return towards God, to consider the Book and the *Sunnat* as the criterion for determining what is right and what is wrong and to keep the ideal of truth before them but the exaggerated estimation of their followers, based on their erudition, courage of conviction and critcism, their selflessness and sacrifice, and the cult of personality, led them towards formation of groups and sects and they went on getting distant from the realm and the base of the *Ummat*, getting suspicious and disgruntled with the *Ulama* of the day and the reformers and losing the capacity and desire to gain advantage from them.

This state of affairs generally overtakes a party whose development and evolution and its mental make-up centres round the personality of one individual, his thinking, ideas and investigations and in whose own mental or religious discipline, no effective element, personality or institution had a hand. The situation worsens when because of the writings of the founder (written only for the purpose of criticising contemporary *Ulama* and thinkers or for assessing the worth of parties), or exaggerated and spirited preachings and exhortations of his followers in their support and assistance, the programme includes, wittingly or unwittingly, negation and often ridicule and censure of the tremendous efforts made by right thinking and erudite *Ulama*, preachers and servants of Islam to accompalish some thing great, or to offset any great calamity or who propagated Islam on an extensive scale, or undertook the job of rectfication and purification of *nafs* and consolation of hearts. The intellectual and academic connection of this *Jama'at* with sincere and well-meaning people outside it, got weaker and weaker and then ceased altogether and it began to live in the shell of the literature of its founder. If within it are not produced thinkers and litterateurs of similar stature, and it lives within its closed walls, it would not get fresh air from outside nor fresh thinking, of direct deduction from the Book and *Sunnat*, which by very nature of things, must be a continuous process. As a result, instead of giving out new shoots and flowering and retaining its freshness and growth, its tree started wilting and withering and dried up to its great detriment. It deprived itself of the great goodness which had spread over the entire community, beyond the limitations of time and space, and which had appeared, time and again, in every age, in every country, institution and group on the basis of correct beliefs and sincerity. Depriving itself of this goodness and confining itself within the arena drawn up by itself, it has done injustice to itself.

The sincere thinkers and men of learning belonging to the *Jama'at* should reflect over this and should keep on assessing the *Jama'at* from this angle and try to rescue it from this state of affairs.

This book is a humble effort by way of extending invitation to them to ponder and reflect and to evaluate themselves—

'We are responsible only to convey the right thing.'

★★★

BIBLIOGRAPHY

1.	Abu Yusuf, Imam,	Kitab ul-Khiraj, Egypt, 1302 A. H.
2.	Ahmad ibn Hanbal, Imam,	Musnad Imam Ahmad.
3.	Alusi, Allama Shahab Uddin ... As-Saiyid,	Tafsir Ruh-ul Mani.
4.	Bukhari, Abu Abdullah, Muhammad ibn Ismail,	Sahih Bukhari, Delhi, 1354 A. H.
5.	Dehlawi, Shah Wali Ullah,	Izalatul Khifa, Delhi.
6.	Al-Huzaibi, Allama Hasan Ismail,	Duwatun la Quzat.
7.	Al-Hakim, Abi Abdullah b. ... Muhammad b. Abdur Rahman,	Mustadrak lil Hakim.
8.	Ibn Hazm, Allama Abu Muhammad b. Ali,	Al-Ihkam fi Usul il-Ahkam, Maktaba Sa'a-data, Egypt.
9.	Ibn Majah, Abu Abd'illah Muhammad b. Yazid,	Sunan Ibn Majah, Cairo, 1373 A. H.
10.	Ibn Kathir, Hafiiz Imad Uddin Abul Fida Ismail ibn Umar,	Tafsir Ibn Kathir, Maktaba Dar Andulus.
11.	Ibn Qayyim, Hafiz	(i) A'ylam al-Muwaqqa-'yin, Vol. II. (ii) Zad al Ma'ad, Egypt, 1324 A. H.

12. Ibn Taimiyah, Shaikh-ul-Islam Ahmad,
(i) Majmua Fatawah Shaikh-ul-Islam Ibn Taimiyah, Vol. XIX, Egypt. 1326 A. H.
(ii) Al-'Abudiyah, Al-Maktaba al-Islam, 1963.

13. Malik b. Anas, Imam, Muwatta Imam Malik.

14. Mehr, Ghulam Rasul Mehr ... Saiyid Ahmad Shaheed, Lahore.

15. Muslim b. Hajjaj al-Qushairi, Sahih Muslim, Delhi. N. D.

16. Maududi, Syed Abul Ala,
(i) Four Basic Quranic Terms.
(ii) Tafhim-ul-Quran, Delhi.
(iii) Tafhimat, Vol. I, II.
(iv) A Short History of the Revivalist Movement in Islam, Lahore, 1963.
(v) The Meaning of the Quran, Vol. II, Delhi, 1973.
(vi) Fundamentals of Islam, Delhi, 1979.
(vii) Islami 'Ibadaat per ek Tahqiqi Nazar, Vol. I, Hyderabad.

17. Nadwi, Syed Abul Hasan Ali,
(i) Western Civilization—Islam and Muslims, Lucknow, 1980.
(ii) Saviours of Islamic Spirit, Vol. I, Lucknow, 1976.
(iii) Qadianism, A Critical Study, Lucknow, 1974.

(iv) Islam and the World, Lucknow, 1972,
(v) Islamic Concept of Prophethood, Lucknow, 1916.
(vi) Al-Nabuwatu wal Anbiya fi Zu al-Quran, Lucknow. 1963.
(vii) Seerat Saiyid Ahmad Shaheed, Lucknow, 1980.

18. Qutb Shaheed, Syed, (i) Ma'alimu fit Tariq.
(ii) Fi Zilal al-Quran.

19. Nissai, Ahmad b. Shuaib b. Ali, Al-Sunan.

20. Nomani, Maulana Mohd. Manzoor, Tasawwuf Kya Hai, Lucknow.

21. Sakhawi, Allama, Al-Maqasid ul-Hasanah.

22. Shatibi, Allama Abu Is'haq Al-Muwafiqat, fi Usul as-Shariata.

23. Shaukani, 'Allama, Neil al-Awtar, Vol VI.

24. Tirmidhi, Imam Muhammad b. 'Isa, ... Jame Tirmidhi,Delhi.

25. Wali Uddin, Al-Khatib al-'Umri, ... Mishkat-al-Masabih.

26. Uthmani, Maulana Shabbir Ahmad, Fath-ul-Mulhim Sharh Sahih Muslim, Vol. I.

★★★

www.ingramcontent.com/pod-product-compliance
Lightning Source LLC
Chambersburg PA
CBHW062142160726
48282CB00027B/913